365 Ways
—TO TELL YOU—
You're Special

**Daily Aspirations and Affirmations
to Nourish and Affirm Your Soul**

By
Dilys Sillah

Copyright © 2024 Dilys Sillah

All rights reserved. No part of this publication may be produced, distributed, or transmitted in any form or by any means, including photocopying, recording, or other electronic or mechanical methods, without the prior written permission of the publisher, except in the case of brief quotations embodied in critical reviews and certain other non-commercial uses permitted by copyright law.

First Printed in United Kingdom 2024

Published by Conscious Dreams Publishing
www.consciousdreamspublishing.com

Edited by Elise Abram
Typeset by Amit Dey
Interior Design: Cerys Price

ISBN: 978-1-915522-60-3

Dedication

To The One who loves me deeper than the deepest well… D.C.A. Thank you for being my affirmation.

Affirmation 1

So, you promised yourself you wouldn't do that 'thing' again. 'I will be stronger next time', 'Why am I so stupid?', 'I wish I wasn't so weak'… Sound familiar? Hooray! You're normal! You missed it. You're alive; therefore, you have another chance to get it right today, and if you miss it today, there's always tomorrow. The key is to not stop trying.

'I have the desire and the will to overcome the things I know don't benefit my emotional or mental health and the things that fuel my insecurities and self-doubt. I am going to cheer myself on and imagine life overcoming those things. I know if I want it, I will be it.'

Affirmation 2

Living life without integrity is living life with a ticking time bomb over everything you've gained through dishonest means. We can't change the past, but we absolutely can change the present and the future. It's never too late to do right by our friends, family and ourselves. The words, 'I am sorry, I apologise' are life-changing, lifesaving and relationship-restoring. Say them.

'I take full responsibility without pointing fingers, for the things I've done that have hurt me and others. I want to be better, so I will do better because I am better.'

Affirmation 3

When you look in the mirror, what and who do you see? Does your sight need adjusting? If you're seeing a whole, joyful and content person looking back at you, celebrate him/her… if you're seeing a broken, sad, defeated soul that's unrecognisable, you need to adjust your emotional and mental lens. That person you're looking at just needs to find their way…let's take a walk.

'I've made a few wrong turns and some wrong turns have made me, but I'm in the driving seat now. I'm readjusting my emotional, spiritual, physical and mental GPS: destination RESTORATION! I'm on my way.'

Affirmation 4

'Pride!' sounds like a funny word when you're trying to remain grounded and humble, so let's try 'proud'. Okay. So, we're cheating a little, but it's okay to be proud of yourself and to take pride in the person you're becoming. You may not be who you want to be yet, but you're not who you used to be…You have every reason to be proud of yourself.

'I won't deny how far I've come. It's not been easy, but I've been determined. I want what's best for me. I'm entitled to it, I want it, I deserve it, I'm ready to work for it, and I'm going to get it.'

Affirmation 5

It's okay to ask yourself, 'So, what's going to be different this time? How do I know this time I won't fail?'

The one thing, the ONLY thing we have, is hope. Hold onto it for dear life. Protect it with all you have and guard it with your heart. If you lose it, you lose the power and fuel you need to do life. Dare to hope and dare to dream.

'I am not the first to fail at something, and I won't be the last. I may have failed this time, but I am not a failure. Because I am NOT a failure, I have every right to believe that I will succeed. I have SUCCESS written all over me.'

Affirmation 6

It's okay to be vulnerable! Where is it written that you have to be strong every day? Who told you you had to show up unscathed, unmarked and unmoved by the trauma, setback and pain you suffered? Who told you? You? Him? Her? Or was it Them? Well, you better set the record straight.

'I'm not superhuman, but I am super, and I am human. I will be okay. I don't need anyone's permission before I take care of myself. Today, I'm taking time out to take care of me, even if it means I take 15 minutes a piece to break, breathe and just be throughout the day. I grant myself permission to be vulnerable today.'

Affirmation 7

Today marks a day that had you in mind before the world was formed. There is a God, and He had you in mind to put you in it. You may not have found your place yet, but it's there, and you will find it. This whole time that you've been searching, has brought you a day closer to your date with destiny... keep going; you're doing great.

'I am not a mistake, regardless of how I came into existence. I have purpose. I will fulfil my destiny. I will finish life well and complete the tasks assigned to my life.'

Affirmation 8

Waking up in the morning is a blessing and a privilege denied many. Waking up in the morning for some doesn't feel like a privilege or a blessing; far from it! If that is you, don't despair. What one thing do you have within your control to change how you feel? Do you need help or support? A listening ear? There is always a solution; we just need to know where to find it.

'I have the power to change my emotional circumstances. I will seek help. I will work towards my emotional and mental freedom. I will not stop until I can wake up and feel blessed and privileged. That is my portion. That is my right.'

Affirmation 9

There is a reason why there's only one you. Anything that is a limited edition holds high value. The fact that others may not see the value, or you don't see the value, does not devalue you! You are one of a kind, so be kind. Be kind to you. Don't look down on you. Look up to you because you are fearfully and wonderfully made.

I strive for perfection, though I know I'm far from perfect. I know to strive means 'to make great efforts to achieve or obtain something'. I commit to striving to bring forth the perfect and best version of my limited-edition self from today, without apology.'

Affirmation 10

Coming into this world doesn't always mean we're welcomed with love and open arms. Sometimes, it's with a clenched fist and gritted teeth, but know you can open your arms to yourself. Be the comfort that you need. Be the safe place you need to go to and exhale. Be the peace that you deserve to enjoy today and always…Be…

'I embrace me. I open my arms to that little boy/girl, and I say to you, "It's okay. It wasn't your fault. You were always special. I am special. You were always beautiful. I am beautiful. You were always wanted. I am wanted."'

Affirmation 11

Words are powerful. They have the power to do and undo. To build and tear down. To bring joy or to bring sadness. Words. They hold the power of life and death. Words are so valuable, but they have the power to devalue. What words are you saying over yourself today? Are they encouraging? Empowering? Loving?

'I won't say to myself what I wouldn't say to a loved one, a person in need or a person in pain. I won't say to myself words that wouldn't look good on a friend. I will be patient with me. I am a work in progress.'

Affirmation 12

We may not have all the answers to the challenges we face, but we do have our challenges for a reason. They may seem hard, insurmountable, and even unfair, but can you imagine the sense of pride and achievement if you stayed the course and overcame each and every one of them? You know you CAN do it, right?

'I have a spirit in me that is bigger and mightier than anything out there. I have been, and am being, tried and tested to see what I'm made of. I am not made for failure. I'm not made to give up. I am not made to be defeated. I will work on myself to win every battle.'

Affirmation 13

Life is not a race, neither is it a competition. Your life is unique to you. Your experiences, your tests, your trials of life—so, why compare yourself to anybody? Your destiny and path to happiness and success are not to be compared to anyone. You only have enough gas and driving experience for your lane.

'My journey is as unique as my thumbprint. There is a thumbprint for my life. I'm in the palm of something bigger. A palm of love, grace, success, healing and all the dreams I want realised. I'm covered. I'm okay.'

Affirmation 14

Miracles still happen; all you have to do is believe. There are situations that come about in life when you literally need a miracle, but nothing can happen unless you believe a little, so start to believe in what you can't see but hope for.

'I put my trust outside of myself. My mind is limitless in what it can believe. My mind is limitless in what it can imagine. I choose to dream. I choose to believe in the answers that are above my limited human thinking and intervention.'

Affirmation 15

Old age doesn't guarantee wisdom, nor is youth confirmation of the lack of it. We can all learn from experience. It's the application of what we've learnt that really counts and demonstrates true wisdom.

'Whatever I have gone through in life, I have not gone through in vain. I will make use of the experiences that I have had to guide me in my life moving forward because I am moving forward.'

Affirmation 16

Give of yourself to those who need you, but never lose yourself because you're being used and taken advantage of. Know when to withdraw and draw the line. Love your neighbour as yourself, not more and certainly not less.

'I make wise investments with my time and my emotions. I am happy to help others, but I am not to be used and taken advantage of. No matter who they are, I am happy to draw my boundaries and move on without guilt.'

Affirmation 17

Comparing yourself to anyone is a surefire way to promote feelings of inadequacy. Sometimes, it's hard to stop, especially if you've been compared or pitted against a sibling. Old habits may die hard, but start with writing down all the things that make you uniquely you. You'll be shocked at how amazing you truly are.

'I am one heck of a human being! The heart I have beats only in my chest. The love and goodness that's inside cannot be compared to anyone or anything. The thoughts in my mind are powerful and beautiful. They give me peace so I can experience peace because I focus on uplifting, inspiring and encouraging things.'

Affirmation 18

Conflict isn't nice, but it's a necessary part of adult life. Sure, you face conflict as a kid, but now you have so many things you're aware of and have to consider with adult relationships. How does one walk away without leaving a bomb site behind? Honest words spoken in love is how. Listening to understand and not just to respond, so you can be heard, too.

'My voice has value. I have value. I have the right to be listened to, but I first need to listen and hear myself. What am I really saying? Is it clear? Is it kind? Is it necessary? Yes? Then I will be bold and speak my truth in love and kindness.'

Affirmation 19

Deciding to go on a healing journey takes guts, and it's hard. That moment, you have to confront what is a thorn in your flesh. You can't ignore it, and your movement is impaired because of it. Your emotional movement is restricted, but through the pain, you've purposed to keep going, so keep going. After a while, the pain eases and BOOM! Freedom comes…put your shoes on and start walking.

'I'm embarking on a journey that I am mentally prepared for. I have made the decision to fill my emotional potholes with love, kindness, understanding and anything else that will give me the strength to heal from the things that have hurt me in life.'

Affirmation 20

We are all human, and sometimes, the human side of us is impatient. Sometimes, the human side of us makes decisions to satisfy where we are today by throwing caution to the wind, no thought for the consequences of tomorrow. But tomorrow will come, and we have to be ready.

'I will be ready for my tomorrow, today. Today is what I can see and have control over. Whatever challenges I have today, I am prepared for. Tomorrow's challenges I will meet head-on because today, I am in control, and I will continue to be in control over my thoughts, body and soul.'

Affirmation 21

*C*ompassion never goes out of fashion, and it's something we need to feel, not just for others, but for ourselves. We need to start with self. Be kind to you. Be gentle to you. Be understanding to you. Create space for you. Take time out for you.

'I understand things have not been easy for me, but I'm going to take time out to consciously understand me so I can be a better version of me, so I don't judge me so harshly. I'm going to take my hand and walk me through my experiences so I can be a settled, healed and happier me.'

Affirmation 22

Another day to show up and show out. Everyone is relying on you, and you sometimes wonder if you can live up to everyone's expectations. But really, what expectations do you have for yourself? Are you meeting them? You can, and you will. Nothing is out of reach; just stretch out your hand that bit farther. You'll grab it… it's yours!

'I will be in expectation of seeing and living what I hope for. I can possess what I dream. I have the drive and tenacity to push for what my heart desires and my potential demands.'

Affirmation 23

Whatever you do that keeps you on the straight and narrow mentally and emotionally, keep on doing it! 'If it ain't broke, don't fix it,' as they say. If you have mastered what helps your wellbeing, maybe share it with others who may benefit from your secrets of wellbeing success.

'I choose to be my brother or sister's keeper. I want to invest in the wellness of those around me. The more healed others are, the more my circle is healed. I will consciously bring those that need me on a journey to also own their healing.'

Affirmation 24

Confidence can be learnt. Every lesson requires a willing and teachable student. If the mind is determined to learn, the teacher has an easier job. If we lack confidence, we can learn to be confident by deciding not to fade into the background, by holding our head up, and pushing our shoulders back and walking tall.

'I don't have the spirit of fear but of power, and of love and of a sound mind. My ability and confidence cannot be limited by fear. I am brave, I am bold. I will trust in everything that I have learnt and be confident in the space that I am in, knowing I have what it takes to be here.'

Affirmation 25

Titles should never allow anyone to feel entitled to treat you poorly or make you feel inferior or bad about yourself. Titles come with responsibility, so if anyone's title is making you feel small, afraid or irrelevant, take away that title, and speak up for yourself and stand up for you.

'I am bold and assertive. I have the capacity and the power to advocate for myself. I have a voice, a strong and powerful voice. I speak clearly and articulately to stand up for what is right. I stand up for me because I am important. I am of value. I deserve to be treated well.'

Affirmation 26

What could I do differently today? Something. Anything. One thing I could fix that I'm putting off. Call someone I'm avoiding. Confront something I have been shying away from. One small change is cause for great celebration.

'Small steps are okay. My small steps are never insignificant. Whatever journey I'm on and wherever it is I'm going, I'm getting there. Slow and steady beats on the spot running. I'll arrive soon.'

Affirmation 27

Keep smiling, but don't forget to cry. That brave face you've been putting on, it's understandable. It's commendable. It's admirable. But it's killing you softly. Give yourself space to feel the hurt. It's the only way you can heal.

'I'm allowed to say it cut me deeper than I realised. I don't owe the world or anyone in it bravery. I only owe myself the space to acknowledge my feelings and embrace all of them. I can't heal if I'm not honest about my experiences and what it's done to me. I can look my pain in the eye and tell it it's time to move forward.'

Affirmation 28

The world is waiting for you to shine. You have a responsibility to reach your full potential. Stop doubting yourself. Somebody is waiting for you to manifest what is inside you.

'I will continue to invest in myself. I will keep building my confidence so I can present myself well. I am a gift and an asset to all those I come into contact with. I bring value to the spaces I am in.'

Affirmation 29

People have the right not to like you! People have the right to have an opinion of the person they perceive you to be; it is their prerogative. The real question is: Do you like you? The beauty of liking you, is you, too, can hold whatever opinion you like without having to convince or justify yourself to anyone. Doesn't it feel great to have an opinion like everybody else?

'I know me. I know who I am. I like me. I know I can like me better in certain areas of my life, but I am happy with the person I am, and I can hold my head up high, knowing I am my best friend.'

Affirmation 30

Fear of the unknown is exactly that! A false sense of what is presenting itself as being real. Fear is a weapon that wages war against faith and hope. So what are you going to do? Let a penknife pretending to be a kitchen knife acting like it can do more damage than an axe scare you? Fear is a tree waiting to be cut down… Let's get to work.

'My perception of the problems I am facing cannot be the only perspective. I don't have to have all the answers; I just need to be willing and open to look for the solutions and do something differently. There's nothing I am going through that others haven't gone through. There's nothing I cannot get through. I'm an overcomer.'

Affirmation 31

We all need a little shelter from the hustle and bustle of life. The noise of the outside world can be overwhelming and can make you feel lost and out of control. It's like everything is moving at a hundred miles per hour! Cars, buses, people just whizzing by, yet you are moving in slow motion trying to put one foot in front of the other, but you can't.

'I CAN! I can do anything. I just need to close my eyes for a moment. Breathe and recentre. As I breathe in, I acknowledge my need for calm. As I breathe out, I believe I possess the calm I need to get through this moment. I can visualise everything slowing down to my pace. I have the ability to control my environment. I can go on with my day today, and it will be a great, calm day.'

Affirmation 32

*D*on't let anyone blow out your light. Hold your lamp high, and don't let your oil run out. It's important that you know your light, no matter how small, can always been seen in darkness. Don't give anyone permission to dim it.

'I will see the treasure in me. I will recognise the gifts that I carry inside me. I will humbly acknowledge my worth and not diminish who I am in favour of anyone or anything. I will shine.'

Affirmation 33

Devote time to your own happiness, and don't feel guilty about it. Everybody has the right to be happy. Everybody has the right to have reasons to smile. So, what are you waiting for? Permission to be happy? No problem… I give you permission to be deliriously happy because it is your right. Take it!

'I have no reason to feel I shouldn't be happy. I will make a conscious effort to do the things that bring me joy and will hang around those who make me happy. I promise myself that I will be more intentional about the things that make me smile, and I will do them. I won't wait until tomorrow; I will start today.'

Affirmation 34

Who do you say you are? You may be many things to many people, but who do you say you are? Have you ever taken the time to sit down and do that introspection? We all change over time because, quite simply, life happens. Who are you at this moment? Where has life brought you? Wherever the starts and stops may have been, you are still here and still going. Make sure you are still going strong.

'Wherever I am at this moment, I am at this point for a reason. I will take my time to quietly reflect on me and where I have come. I have done well. I have weathered many storms, and I am just taking a breather until I continue on my way. I am self-reflective, and I am making mental notes of who and where I want to be.'

Affirmation 35

What needs doing today? What have you postponed or put off because of fear or overwhelm? Not opening your letters because you don't know what it says? Avoiding that email because there is a message you're not quite up to reading? Fear of the unknown only has power because of what is unknown, but you know you can face anything if you believe you can. Well, that is all you need to know.

'I don't ever have to feel afraid of information. Whatever I feel I can't cope with, I will find the help and support I need. I can take control over fear by allowing myself to look for the answers to the problems I come across. I am brave. I do not bury my head in the sand. I am responsible, so I take responsibility to find the right solutions. I am not overwhelmed by my problems because I am greater than my fears.'

Affirmation 36

When you're tired, STOP! Stop telling yourself you're not tired, that you're okay and can keep pushing yourself. It is absolutely okay to pull the brakes on friends, family, children, the job, the business—whatever it may be—and just STOP! Be selfish sometimes. You are needed. You are important. You are heavily relied upon, and that is why you need to stop and take care of yourself. You are important, but you aren't irreplaceable, and yet you are. Rest is not for the weak; it's for the strong. Your strength is needed, so take time out and relax. It's okay to stop.

'I know I hold and carry value for the people who matter in my life. I know I need to be full and present to give the very best of myself so I will be the best to myself. I will rest when I am tired. I will allow my mind to be at peace so I can be the best version of me. I will not feel guilty for putting myself first.'

Affirmation 37

'Forgive and forget,' 'Be the bigger person,' they say, but you're hurt and angry and need to be heard. So, you pretend you're over whatever has grieved your heart or your pride, but that pain just won't go away. Acknowledge your hurt, acknowledge your pain, and you can begin to truly forgive and free yourself from the prison of unforgiveness.

'I refuse to be controlled by my feelings. I may not feel like forgiving those who have hurt me and caused me pain, but I can, and I will. As they have moved on with their lives, I choose to move on with mine. My shoulders are not for carrying hurt, pain and offence. I walk tall and travel light. I free everyone I have been holding captive in my heart and in my soul so I can breathe again.'

Affirmation 38

You are allowed down moments… just make sure it's just a moment. The world can survive you putting you first once in a while. You will be okay.

'I will take time out to gather my thoughts and reprioritise. I will take time to re-evaluate the things that need me now, the things that can wait, and the things that don't need me at all. I will not allow anything to have a hold on me that does not serve me. I can let go of things and keep a hold of myself. I am always worth making a priority.'

Affirmation 39

What has your attention? What are you focusing on? It seems it's always the things that cause us to fear that we focus on. Where there's fear, there's also faith. Which side do you want to be on? Feed your mind with a positive narrative. Whatsoever things are true, pure, lovely, noble, of good report – meditate on those things. Your mental health will thank you for it.

'I choose to think of the good and not the bad. I am a winner, and I imagine myself winning in every situation where I have felt fear or defeat or inadequacy. I am fearfully and wonderfully made. I can do all things. I have the strength to overcome all obstacles in my way.'

Affirmation 40

We all want to grow, but growth sometimes means leaving things behind. A job, a church, a place of work, a marriage, a relationship, friends… Growth comes at a cost; it is not free. It can be painful and fill you with so much guilt, but if you don't grow, you don't progress. Stagnancy and never reaching your full potential emotionally, mentally or spiritually does not look good on anyone. Allow yourself to blossom and grow into the person you were designed to be.

'I will not stunt my growth by feeding the weeds of life. Things and people holding me back from reaching my full potential. I will let go, some gently, some not so gently. I will keep my eye on the prize, and that prize is my next level. I am determined to be all I have the power and ability to be.'

Affirmation 41

We all make mistakes. We all have a story to tell. Who hasn't done things they are not proud of? From choice of partners to following unflattering fashion trends and everything in between—been there, done that, worn the T-shirt. Guess what? You are not the only one, so give yourself a break. You are allowed to get it wrong. Your past is your past, so give yourself a pass.

'I have made mistakes. I am human. I have done and said things that I am not proud of. I have made bad choices, and they have affected me and others, but I am ready to make a decision today. I am ready to leave the past where it belongs and embrace my future.'

Affirmation 42

Everything around us tells us how great it is to fall in love and live happily ever after, but nobody really tells you what to do when it all goes wrong. You get stuck and can't seem to see past your pain, but maybe that's the problem. Walk through the pain and embrace all the emotions that go with it. The only way to get past the pain is to get through the pain.

'I am not my experience. I can heal from the hurt and confusion of a love lost. I can move forward from betrayal and disappointment. I am a magnet for pure, real and healthy love. Because I deserve to be in a healthy union, I can let go of unhealthy connections. I am worthy of good, wholesome love.'

Affirmation 43

Because life happens to all of us, it has the power to change us in so many different ways, some for good and some for bad. Certain experiences can make us bitter or make us better; the choice is ours. When we choose to grow from our experiences, not everybody will celebrate us. Strength is frightening when people are used to seeing you weak, but that's okay. Nobody needs to be convinced by your evolution.

'I am a person of divine purpose. I am unapologetic about the strength I have to overcome the challenges in my life. I will not shrink or fade into the background to make anybody comfortable with my past weakness or timidity. I have grown, and I have evolved. I own my newfound voice, presence and power.'

Affirmation 44

Love has many meanings, and none of them mean love is supposed to hurt. Love should never hurt you mentally, physically, emotionally or spiritually. What love is is patient. Love is kind; it does not envy or boast, it is not self-seeking. Love is not easily angered, and love does not keep account of wrongdoing. If the 'love' that you are in doesn't do these things, then it is not love.

'I choose to love myself. I choose to be all these things to me. I choose to set the example for others on how I am to be loved and appreciated. I am an excellent demonstrator of what self-love looks like.'

Affirmation 45

Sometimes, time can move so fast; before you know it, another year has passed. All the people you promised to stay in touch with countless promises to improve on your health, spend more time with the family, and so much more, and it doesn't happen for good reason. But regret makes it important enough to notice you didn't do any of the things your heart desired.

'I am going to enjoy my present. I am going to take in the little things and revel in the things that make me happy. I will be deliberate in making time for the things that bring me joy because I am worth it.'

Affirmation 46

Do something nice for a neighbour. Sometimes, the unlikeliest people are in the greatest need our kindness. Take a moment to look around and see who might need a helping hand and give it. You and your community will be all the better for it. It doesn't matter if you are the only one; it only takes one.

'I inhabit all that is good and kind about humanity. I will show that all is not lost in this world by being the answer to someone's needs. I will show neighbourly love to someone who needs it.'

Affirmation 47

Time can be both kind and unkind to us, depending on what you want time to do for you. If you have grey hairs popping up, or your baby is starting nursery, your kids are off to university, or you can't do the things you once did, embrace the change. Time is being good to you. Time is giving you a story to tell.

'At whatever stage I am at, in whatever state I am in, I am grateful for the gift of life. I have so much I can look at and be grateful for. Time is my best friend, and I will use her wisely because she has been good to me. She has given me today, and I am grateful.'

Affirmation 48

In a time when everybody is so busy, and we are taught to be more and more self-serving, where do you go for support and to be heard? Is there anyone whose shoulder you can lean or cry on? Yes? That's great! No? They say you have to be the person or friend you want others to be to you. Who can rely on you?

'I will be the friend I want others to be to me. I will make myself available to those in need because I am sowing seeds that will bear fruit for me. I will make wise decisions in where I sow those seeds. I am discerning, and I am wise. I will sow my seed on good ground because I am good ground. I will get what I give out. I will be surrounded by goodness when I am in need of a genuine friend.'

Affirmation 49

We all have different destinies and assignments on this earth. It is folly to compare your life to anyone else's. So, you started out together with your friends from university, and they are doing better than you, or you started out at the same job as your colleague, and they got the big promotion, or you started trying for a family, and you've had no luck yet. I understand. It's hard, and you feel left behind. Please don't. Life is not a race, and tickets to success aren't handed out on a first-come-first-served basis. However, it's a grace and favour thing that's extended to all if you stay on course. Just wait your turn. Have faith. It's coming.

'I am focused on my future and my destiny. I am the only one who can fulfil it. My life's experiences, past and present, are shaping me for that amazing future I have my eye on. In the meantime, I will celebrate those who have gone before me because I have a pure heart and soul that appreciates the blessings and good fortunes of others.'

Affirmation 50

Who are your friends? Show me your friends, and I'll show you your character. How true or false is this? Who are you hanging with? Are they a reflection of who you are or who you want to be? If you want to be held accountable and stay on track morally, mentally, professionally, spiritually—watch the company you keep. Indeed, bad company corrupts good character. Be wise in who you call friend.

'I attract good people with clean hearts and souls in my space. I am a person who is intentional about the company I keep. I am of high value. I treat people well. I hold space for myself and others. I do not attract disloyalty because I am loyal.'

Affirmation 51

Sometimes, past experiences make us judge people and situations badly. I know—we're only human, so our views can only be expressed from what we have gone through. But guess what? Other people do exactly the same. It's called 'self-preservation'. We do our best to protect ourselves from getting hurt, so we rush to put up the barriers to stop pain and hurt coming in… but why don't you take a chance on life? You might be pleasantly surprised.

'I will not let fear stop me from opening up myself to receive good things. I will not block my blessings because of past hurts and disappointments. I will take a chance, and if it doesn't go my way, I will not let it cripple me or make me bitter. I will learn from it, take responsibility if I need to, and use my experience for my growth.'

Affirmation 52

Love must always start with self. Charity begins at home. You cannot give what you don't have. Take time to get to know yourself better. Think about the things that make you happy, things that are important to you and things that make you smile. Love on yourself and spoil yourself. That way, you can show others how to love on you.

'I love me. I accept me for who I am. I am worthy of love. I deserve to be loved. If I have to, I will wait for love. I show up as a person who is balanced and secure in my emotions. I love myself enough to only offer myself to those who appreciate, respect and love me back.'

Affirmation 53

Wherever you find yourself, make sure it's a safe space. Whether it's work, at a party, in a relationship, amongst a group of friends, at a religious gathering or even on social media, make sure your space is safe. People are not designed to be battered emotionally or mentally, so a space that makes you anxious takes away your confidence or belittles you is not a space for you. You are your own gatekeeper. Don't sleep on duty; stand and guard the gates well.

'I will only go where I am celebrated. If I feel unsafe or my sense of peace is threatened, I will confidently put myself first and remove myself from such spaces. I deserve peace and calmness to be around me. I am a carrier of peace, so I will always expect peace and enjoy peace in return.'

Affirmation 54

*B*reaking harmful habits can be really hard. We repeat what's familiar, even though we know it doesn't serve us, like a bad relationship. It takes guts to call time on something we had high hopes for. It's okay to let things go. You are special, and what is not good for you, you must release.

'If I put my mind to it, I can picture a life without depending and leaning on things that impede my ability to stand on my own. I do not need a crutch. I do not need anything in my life that takes away from my ability to be strong.'

Affirmation 55

The familiar is always comfortable. It does not challenge us to heights of excellence. The familiar will tell you it's okay to settle and not to want more, but you can have more in this life if you desire more. Just take a deep breath and take the plunge into the unknown. You will land on safe ground.

'I know I was meant for more than I am experiencing now. I know I can have more than I have out of life now. I am not afraid to take a leap of faith and expect to land safely where my destiny has been calling me.'

Affirmation 56

When you look around your environment, what do you see? Order? Things in their rightful place or clutter and disorganisation? Sometimes, the space we're in is trying to tell us to get organised or develop the discipline to be orderly. If your surroundings are symbolic of what's going on inside, take one item at a time, breathe and start packing, sweeping, wiping, clearing; your mind will be better for it.

'I have a clear mind because I will take my time to do a mental clear out of unhealthy thoughts in an orderly, organised way. I will pace myself. I will be patient and kind to me. I will put my thoughts in order so I can make sound judgements and decisions about the clutter in my head. I am capable and able of finding order and balance, inwardly and outwardly.'

Affirmation 57

Don't always rely on your own wisdom. We are only as good as the experiences we have been through or witnessed, and sometimes, this isn't enough to allow for the best judgements. Seek knowledge and wisdom from wise and sound sources and see how much you can enhance the quality of the decisions you make and your thought processes.

'I am open to hearing and appreciating the views and wisdom of others who have gone before me and can help me to be better in the areas I need help. I don't have to burden myself to find all the answers. If I follow the road of wisdom and wise counsel, I, too, will be the wisdom and wise counsel others seek.'

Affirmation 58

Sometimes, we find ourselves drowning in life's troubles, and there doesn't appear to be a way out. We seem to go round in circles looking for peace, a way out, a sign, even, but there's nothing there. It's in those times we need to just be still. Take in the moment and just be. In the calmness of the moment and with a peaceful spirit, answers will come.

'I will close my eyes and block out the noise that affects my ability to think strategically and my power to overcome the things that are troubling me. As I breathe, I release control and serenity over myself and my circumstances. I can change my world.'

Affirmation 59

Love is a word that comes and goes. We all want to have it, but do we know how to give it? Love is most beautiful when it's given freely and does not seek or demand anything in return.

'I want to be the person who shows someone love today. I will be the solution to someone's problem. I want to be someone's answered prayer. I believe in the law of sowing and reaping, and I believe I will receive the love I put out when I need it.'

Affirmation 60

When you have been told by a parent, a loved one, or someone you care about that you are not enough, you tend to believe that lie. The fact is you are enough and more than enough for those who recognise a great soul when they encounter one. It's not what people say about you; it's what you know about yourself.

'I will not empower anyone to disempower me by their words. It doesn't matter who it is, how long they've known me, if they know me. I know me. I will cancel, erase and strike out any opinion of me that contradicts the truth of my essence.'

Affirmation 61

Hope is the lifeline to knowing better days lie ahead whenever you're in a place that looks like a dead end or a maze. Hope becomes the direction that will lead you to the light at the end of the tunnel.

'I will keep hope alive because I know that no situation is permanent. I make a choice to visualise the solution to my challenges and problems, and I see me winning every time because I am a winner.'

Affirmation 62

The greatest power that stops us from healing is silence. Fear underpins that silence to ensure that we are stuck in a place of pain and rawness. But if you could only start with a whisper then reach that crescendo, healing will come because you have given your pain a voice. You have the right to be heard because your pain matters. You matter.

'I am not afraid. Fear has no hold over me. I will fear no one. I will fear nothing. I will be bold. I will stand tall and speak my truth. I will be heard. Yes, my voice matters.

Affirmation 63

The seasons of life are ever-changing, and our lives are no different. There is a time and a season for everything and for everyone. So long as we are prepared for the season we are in, we can weather any storm, the scorching sun, the high winds and the heavy rains.

'In time, in its due season, all the things my heart desires, I will receive. I will be patient. I will not be anxious. I will live life in wholeness, in peace and with calm expectation to receive those desires.'

Affirmation 64

They say the truth hurts, but it doesn't have to. Kindness and truth can go together when spoken in love. Why is this important? It's important because if you speak truth in kindness to yourself, you will do so to others. What a great feeling to be a person others can run to for realness wrapped in kindness and compassion.

'In a world full of untruths and deception, I will be that safe haven, exhibiting kindness to others with my words. I will be honest in my opinions, advice and views. Kindness and compassion are second nature to me.'

Affirmation 65

Friendships are great when they are genuine. Friendships teach us about loyalty, commitment, and sacrifice. Somehow, we believe the length of time we have known a person signifies the greatness of that friendship. Wrong! The length of time of a friendship is not what makes it solid or good. Are they there when you need them, and do they have your back? Know your worth, and walk away from long-term liabilities. You have the right to have good souls in your camp who value genuine friendship.

'I will not cast my pearls before swine. I place a high value on the friendship I give. I will let go of friends whom I have outgrown to make way for new connections for this season in my life. I embrace change, and I embrace new friendships that will be a blessing to me.'

Affirmation 66

It doesn't matter how much money we have; true wealth is measured by how healthy we are. We can chase all the contracts, cars, money, big businesses all we want; if we aren't well enough to enjoy it, it means nothing. The best investments with the greatest returns are those that involve our health.

'My body is a temple, and I will look after the one body I have. I will think about what I put in my body. I will be deliberate about all elements of my health. What I eat and what I drink. I will nurture and feed my body for the better. Health, strength and wellness is mine.'

Affirmation 67

There's always a little bit of people pleaser in us. That bit of praise we hope for, the reassurance and affirmation from others to make us feel good. That's okay; just don't get too used to it. You don't want to be lost if you don't get it.

'I am my greatest fan. I know I can do whatever I put my mind to. I feel good about myself, and I am confident in me.'

Affirmation 68

It is okay to be silent. Not everything requires a response. Sometimes, indeed, silence is golden. There are many things that demand our energy, but we need to be mindful of what we lend our energy to. If we can let it go, and it does not compromise us in any way, then let it go. Your energy is needed for people and things that edify you.

'I am peaceful. I am calm, and I choose my battles wisely. I will not fall into places that upset my spirit. I will not engage with people or situations that take tranquillity away from me.'

Affirmation 69

Hearing things about ourselves can hurt; it doesn't really matter whether what has been said is true or not. Whenever we are spoken about in a way that is not positive, it can make us feel insecure, judged, and condemned, but there is a confidence that comes that allows you not to be bothered because you know who you are.

'Truth always prevails. I will trust in the sincerity of my character to speak for me. In time, all that is hidden will be revealed. Wherever I need vindication, I will find it.'

Affirmation 70

Being content with life can be a beautiful thing, but don't ever feel guilty for wanting more. You have every right to want the best of everything. Your heart's desires are there for a reason. Those desires are there to spur you on to get what you want out of life, so what are you waiting for?

'I am going for it. It's scary, and I may not know exactly what I'm doing, but I'm following my heart. My heart will lead me where it wishes, and I will be happy.'

Affirmation 71

Perspective. It's not just what happens to us; it's how we perceive the experience. A glass half empty or half full can mean we don't have enough water to quench our thirst, or it could mean we are thankful we are not as thirsty as we were before we had half a glass of water. Our mindset can set us up for success or failure. Let's choose success.

'I will think positively about every situation. I will look for the good and not just see the bad. In all situations, there are lessons to be learnt. I will be open to believing things will work out for me, and I will use my experience to overcome.'

Affirmation 72

Gratitude is not just a feeling; it's a lifestyle. There is so much to be grateful for. We may need to remind ourselves from time to time about what those things are, but in the quiet stillness of our thoughts, we must remember that life is a gift that we are blessed to have.

'I am thankful and grateful for all that I am and all that I will be. I am grateful for where I stand today and for the path of my journey. My heart is full of gratitude for how far I've come and how far I have the power to go.'

Affirmation 73

What do most people want? Riches, happiness, good health? That's people, but what do you want? Different people want different things, and sometimes, different people want the same things but at different times. Before investing yourself in a relationship, make sure your desires align with the right people at the right time.

'I am clear on where I am at this juncture of my life. I will not compromise on my wants and needs. I will be intentional about my connections. I will not short-change myself or others by settling. I am worthy to receive my heart's desires.'

Affirmation 74

Our thoughts are important. What we feed our thoughts show up in how we deal with life. Negative and bad thoughts will impact how we make decisions and how we problem-solve. Let's be mindful of what we watch, who and what we listen to, and the things we read. Let them be uplifting, edifying and positive. One of the most precious gifts we have is our minds; protect it.

'I will guard my mind and be mindful of what I let in. Anything that causes my mind to be unsettled, I will close the gates to it. Anything that causes anxiety or fear, I will close the gates to it. Anything that promotes self-hate or self-doubt, I will close the gates to it. I am in charge. I will continue to have a sound and settled mind.'

Affirmation 75

Today is a day of rest. Rest from stress, rest from anxiety, rest from anything that does not cause you to smile. Take control of every situation that is troubling you, and just…breathe. Allow yourself the time to rest from the demands of life, even if it's just for a minute. Rest.

'I will take ten minutes of my day and just sit in quiet. I will close my eyes and imagine myself in a safe and tranquil space, and I will rest. My mind, my body and my soul. I will make time for me to just be.'

Affirmation 76

Make friends with time. She can be harsh, but most of the time, she's kind. She gives of herself for you to determine what kind of relationship you want with her. Make time for her, and she will make time for you.

'I use my time wisely. I am intentional about the time I have and the time I am given. I am spontaneous, but I also take time to put plans to my thoughts and ideas. I am positioning myself to see the benefits of my time being used wisely; regret will never have a hold of me.'

Affirmation 77

Most people don't like confrontation, but confrontation is part of being an adult. Some situations won't sort themselves out unless you say or do something. Things that trouble you will rarely just go away. You will need to put on your big-person pants and get on with it. You can do it!

'I have the right to draw my boundaries, say how I feel and make my feelings known. I will not shy away from speaking up for myself. I will not allow situations to eat away at me inside. I have the right words to speak at the right time. I am a good advocate for myself.'

Affirmation 78

Money, indeed, is the root of all evil, but money is not evil. It can be the answer to many things, and being able to meet the needs of others is one of them. Caring enough about others who are less fortunate than us is admirable; helping others is even better. The help we give to others will come back to us, pressed down, shaken together and running over.

'I will consciously and actively look for opportunities to give to others. I can give of my money, compassion, time and wisdom. Because I give these things to others, I can expect my needs to be met in the same way.'

Affirmation 79

Sometimes, it's good to let off steam. Scream, shout, cry. There are times when this little display will release tension and stress, and surprisingly, put you back in control. It's okay to go crazy once in a while.

'I don't have to pretend I'm okay. I can express my emotions when I need to. I will not tell myself I am okay when I am not okay because it's okay not to be okay.'

Affirmation 80

It feels great to reach the milestones we set out to achieve. From getting that degree to buying that house or car. Whatever it is, celebrate your win. It's okay to pat yourself on the back and say, 'Well done. I did it!'

'I celebrate my wins. I will not downplay the cost of achieving my goals. It was not easy. It was not handed to me. I worked for it. I am blessed by it. I will enjoy my achievements.'

Affirmation 81

No friendship should feel like a prison. If it's not meeting your needs and taking away from you, move on. It's unfair to you to remain in a friendship that's not friendly. Your time should never be spent marking time instead of making good use of time by investing in the right relationships.

'I will not be sentimental about decisions I need to make about the friends I choose to let go. I am an adult, and I have complete autonomy over who I allow in my circle. I will not feel guilty for wanting the best for me.'

Affirmation 82

When was the last time you cried? I mean, really cried? Apart from the fact that it's a necessary expression of emotion, it's actually very good for you. It releases toxins and relieves stress, and research has found that in addition to being self-soothing, crying releases oxytocin and endorphins that help you feel better. So, go and grab some tissues, and just let it all out.

'I have nothing to prove to anyone. I am allowed to cry when I need to. I do not need permission to express my hurt or pain. I will not feel ashamed because I need to cry. Being a man/woman will not stop me from expressing my emotions. I will not be shamed into silence. I will shed my tears to aid my healing.'

Affirmation 83

We are often not encouraged to listen or trust our intuition because we want to see and have evidence of everything before we believe, but your instincts are there for a reason. They are your guide and protector. Listen to that voice inside you. It knows what it's talking about.

'I trust my gut. I do not need to justify why I will obey the voice inside me. I trust that voice, and if I'm wrong, it doesn't matter. I just need more time to practice and develop that gift of discernment.'

Affirmation 84

'What doesn't break you makes you stronger'… apparently. But what doesn't break you can leave you cracked and dented or out of shape. Don't put up with pain or disappointment just because it's expected. Until you feel strong, reach out and get the help and support you need.

'When I don't feel strong, I won't pretend I am. I won't look for cliches to invalidate what I am going through. I will be present in the moment and gather strength with words of affirmation and the belief that things will be okay.'

Affirmation 85

$\mathcal{E}$verything isn't supposed to make sense. Some things in life will forever remain a mystery, like why we have to lose things and people we love, especially at the point that we love them the most. Believe all things will work out for your good. Only then can you make way for what needs to be birthed.

'I will mourn my losses. I will take time to revel in the joy and pain of what has escaped me. I will make a way through the pain to let light in. My life is light and not darkness, so I will shine. In time, in spite of it all, I will shine.'

Affirmation 86

Tasks that take so much out of us, we would rather not do, so we put them off until later…and later never comes. We go around frantic and flustered because the pressure is on and the anxiety is at its peak. Everything, at some point, is important, but you are always important, so give yourself time to respond to the demands of life and allow for calm to set the pace.

'I will avoid placing myself in stressful situations. I will actively learn how to manage my time and responsibilities. I am beyond capable of putting my house, work and life in order to create order.'

Affirmation 87

Nobody has the right to remind you of your past, especially if you have moved on from it. It takes a lot to overcome trauma, drink, drugs or anything that could have destroyed you. You have the right to forget and enjoy the future you have created.

'I am a new creation. I am not my past. I am delivered from the things that have held me down, and I will remain delivered. I am the only one that has the key to unlock memories from my past. I choose to keep that part of life under lock and key. I have moved on.'

Affirmation 88

It's good to retreat and create 'me time', but the various demands of life can make it hard. Be intentional about tending to yourself, and be there for you as much as you are for others.

'Making time for me is important for my mental health. I will look for those moments where I can relax and enjoy peace of mind and peace in the space I create.'

Affirmation 89

*C*reating positive habits is a great way to keep you physically, mentally and spiritually on track when you are committed to something. Repetition is only madness if the result you're getting is not the one you're looking for. Consistency always wins the race, so never stop at being fabulously consistent.

'Slow and steady wins the race. I will focus and be mindful of distractions. I have the strength of mind to stay the course until I achieve all I set out to.'

Affirmation 90

Rewriting history is possible. History has a habit of repeating itself. If we are able to readjust our vision and go back and see the negative patterns of our lives, we can put them right. We have the authority to determine how our story is going to end.

'I will be kind to myself whilst I take responsibility for the negative things that have become a pattern in my life. Revelation brings change, and I am ready to change for the better. I am ready to be the best version of me.'

Affirmation 91

Don't ever settle to be anyone's second choice. You're good enough to be number one. If people don't see your value, don't force them to! Not everyone has an eye for rare quality goods.

'I will never waste my time forcing others to see my worth or to accept me. I will never devalue myself by trying to prove that I am worthy. I do not need to prove the obvious.'

Affirmation 92

There are many roads to success in this life, so failure shouldn't be the road we walk. If we take our time to put plans in place, seek good counsel and advice from those who have gone before us, we can make it.

'Nothing good comes easy, so I will not be afraid to give my all. I won't look for shortcuts for long-term success or gains. I believe that my labour will not be in vain because I rightly apply the laws of success to my life.'

Affirmation 93

Happiness can be a state of mind, but it can also be a decision. Sometimes, there are so many reasons to be down, you literally have to self-talk and decide what mood you're going to have today. So, make a decision, but please make it a good one.

'I embrace happiness as my mood today. I will focus on that word. I will smile and battle sadness away today. Today, I take a hold of my emotions and not let my emotions take a hold of me. I will go to that happy place in my mind and stay there.'

Affirmation 94

Taking care of the old isn't just about the elderly, though that's a great starting point and an investment in our own futures. But the old signifies experience, service, purpose. From old friendships to old shoes, all have played a part in how we have benefited from that person or thing standing the test of time. Show appreciation; it is the highest form of thanks.

'I appreciate all the things in my life that have stood the test of time. My relationships, clothes and shoes that bring back memories of when they were first bought and have served me well. I embrace the new, but I appreciate and am grateful for the old.'

Affirmation 95

Resilience is a powerful word reserved for powerful people who refuse to give up. It's a word that those with the power rarely even realise they have it to use it. That person is you; yes, YOU! You have come so far; you cannot give up now.

'I have the desire and ability to keep pressing in. To stand my ground and to keep believing I will win every battle I am in. I am made of steel. I will not break. I will stay the course and come out victorious. I am resilience.'

Affirmation 96

Forgiving a wrong or an injustice can be one of the hardest things to do. When it's a situation where you aren't the only person who has been hurt, and others will judge your choice to forgive or see your forgiveness as a betrayal, think long and hard about what you really want. It's entirely your decision to forgive. If it will make you feel better, do it.

'I know it takes guts to stand by my convictions and make the decision to move on. I will understand that others have the right to their feelings but not the right to control mine. I will think and act in the best interest of my conscience and wellbeing.'

Affirmation 97

Always set your own standards of integrity. Your needs will always test the depths of your values and standards. Will you cheat because you need a promotion, lie because unfaithfulness is beckoning, steal because you put your needs above another? Nobody is perfect, but imperfection can be worked on. You can be better, so let's do better.

'I treat others with honesty and openness. I do only that which I would want done to and for me. I show up as a person who is always trustworthy and honest. I am a safe person to be around. I am a safe person to be with. I am a haven.'

Affirmation 98

*P*atience, indeed, is a virtue. It's one of the greatest things we can possess. Why? Because when we are not in a hurry for experiences or things, we are able to hold greater power to think strategically and make better decisions from a place not governed by desperation. We are more powerful when patient.

'I am able to make decisions from a good place and not from a place of hurt, anger, desperation or disappointment. I think clearly, I act responsibly, I execute my decisions with calm authority.'

Affirmation 99

Be excited about life. Find something that makes your heart skip a beat. Find something that makes you want to get up in the morning. This life will give you what you give it permission to give. Have a word with your situation and watch it begin to obey the command of excitement and greatness being released into your world.

'I have the ability, knowledge and power to make my life one I want to live. I have control over my thoughts to manifest the life I desire and the life I deserve.'

Affirmation 100

If only we could recognise the magic inside each one of us and the beautiful gifts that we possess to make this world a better place. If only we could realise that we are not the pain we have experienced but the passion we have yet to express.

'I choose, from now on, to fearlessly express the gifts inside me. I will not focus on my shortcomings, but I will focus on all things good and beautiful about my existence and what I have to give this world.'

Affirmation 101

What is taking your time? What has taken your attention? Be mindful of what or who that is. If it's stopping you from focusing on what will benefit you, take your time back; it's too precious to waste.

'I will not fix my attention on things that distract me and keep me preoccupied with what will be of no benefit to me. I will be conscious about what and who takes my time. My time is precious, and so am I.'

Affirmation 102

People fear you. Your confidence and greatness can cause fear in others, but that's their problem. Too often, we don't know the awesomeness that surrounds us, and we end up dumbing down who we are to accommodate what we should never have entertained, and that is the insecurities of others.

'I am a tower. I am a powerhouse. I will recognise daily that I am a force to be reckoned with. I will not diminish myself in my own eyes. I am great.'

Affirmation 103

What is your reality? The things we see around us? What we feel? What we experience? They may be facts, but are they truth? Experiences in life can break you and often do—another fact! But truth says you have the ability to write your own story, regardless of what life and circumstance say how you are supposed to turn out.

'I am not my experience. Many have fallen and been broken by what they have gone through. I will not allow any event in my life, past, present or future, to define who I am. My truth is that I am above all the pain, disappointments, and setbacks. I define who I am, not my experiences.'

Affirmation 104

Most people want to be the ones to lead, but true leaders are great at being of service. You do better to learn how and what the people you wish to lead need so you can be great at serving them. It's here where you learn humility and sacrifice: the greatest attributes of a great leader.

'I will learn how to serve others to enhance how I can lead. How I serve is my way of taking on the responsibility to lead and guide those who depend on me now and in the future. I will be approachable, humble and willing to be all that is needed for me to lead with strength and integrity because I have what it takes.'

Affirmation 105

Change your attitude and mindset if you want a different result to the challenges you have been facing in your life. If your mindset is negative, then, no doubt, you will struggle to see a positive outcome. Focus on positive things, and see your faith rise and tell you things will be okay because you have told yourself they will.

'I am in total control of what I see. I am in total control of what I feel. I will not allow the external things to block my vision of what is on the horizon. I am focusing on and walking towards the light. Everything concerning me will be more than okay.'

Affirmation 106

Where do you invest your time? What takes up most of it? Do you know that what you spend time on says a lot about the things that are important to you or what you prioritise? Take a moment and think about what that is.

'I will take time to look at what is really important to me and what should take my time and focus. I will not allow the people and things I love to be second best to things that take my time that aren't really important. Time is precious; I value it because I am valuable, and so are the people I love.'

Affirmation 107

Be consistent with your actions if you want the results you're looking for. Consistency is what wins the race, not wishes. It will take sacrifice and good, old-fashioned grit and stubbornness to get to where you have set your heart to get to. Keep going; you can, and you will get there.

'I will give up whatever is acting as a hinderance to me achieving my goals and what I set my sights on. I will dig deep and not give in to my desires to quit because I am not a quitter! I am a fighter, and I will reach the finish line.'

Affirmation 108

Take a moment to see how far you've come. Whether in character, career or whatever else, take a moment to celebrate how far you've come. You could have quit! You could have thrown in the towel, but you didn't. You did good. Give yourself a round of applause; many didn't make it this far.

'It has not been easy, and I know others have it way harder than I do, but I will not downplay my achievement because of that. If I have come this far, I have proved I have it in me to be a winner, always.'

Affirmation 109

It's always good to find ways to keep our minds active and curious. Find something new to do. Try something you've never done before that pushes you out of your comfort zone. Challenge you and see what you can do because you can do anything.

'I will create the space to grow in every area of my life. If I want to learn something new, I won't be afraid to. I will commit to it. I will open my mind to new adventures and enjoy the ride along the way.'

Affirmation 110

Superstitions have been here from time immemorial, and many people have them. Whatever yours may be, make sure they're positive and nothing that leaves you fearful or confessing negativity over yourself and others. Your thoughts, your words, are what will make or break you. Speak goodness over you and your environment, and it will come good.

'I dictate what my existence will be. I am not afraid of what I cannot see or feel. I am present and in control of what comes into my mental, emotional and spiritual space. I will not give my authority to anyone or anything in these areas of my life.'

Affirmation 111

'Don't worry, be happy!' You know the song. But let's be honest: it's easier said than done. So many of us have good reason to worry, so we do. We do it to the point of making ourselves ill with sleepless nights and loss of appetite, all in the name of worry. You were never created for worry but for peace and happiness. Let that be your counterargument when worry comes knocking.

'I will take a step back and objectively look at what is trying to take my mind and emotions on a ride I don't want to go on. I will pull the brakes and steer my thoughts into a positive place, a place where I can think clearly and without noise. There is a solution and answer to my worries. I will seek them, and I will find them.'

Affirmation 112

Hope for tomorrow is always there. Some days can have you so down you can barely lift your head, but the truth is that vision of a breakthrough will keep you going when nothing else will. Never surrender your hope, never give up your faith. No problem or situation is bigger than either.

'I will walk into my peace. I may stop along the way, but I will get to the place that will be the evidence of my hope. I know, without any doubt, that I am always going to come back to this place whenever I need to.'

Affirmation 113

Thank those who helped you along your journey. Nobody is an island. People share their life experiences and knowledge to push us to where we are destined to be. Recognise them and appreciate them. A heart of thanks is a heart, indeed. It will come full circle as others recognise the part you played in their story. Keep the gratitude going.

'My heart is a magnet for all things that are good and pure because I hold gratitude and respect for those who have helped me along the way. I will continue to attract good things by sowing into the life of others and seeing them grow as I grow.'

Affirmation 114

We all have expectations of others and them of us, but if those expectations aren't managed, we can overburden people and they us. Never expect from others what you cannot give, and if you can, never assume it will be reciprocated or appreciated.

'I will always be gracious and not impose unreasonable expectations on others. I will give without expecting anything in return. I will give freely because it is my choice to help others. In my giving is where I have my reward, and that is enough.'

Affirmation 115

Communication is a great key to possess for healthy relationships. Being open, clear and consistent with your wants and needs really helps others to know how to respect your boundaries. Don't ever be afraid to set them.

'I have the right to protect my emotional and mental space. I don't ever have to apologise for saying what does not feel good to me. I am responsible for my wellbeing. I will defend it at all costs. I am worth being treated well by all.'

Affirmation 116

It's a good thing to be discerning but not so good to be overly suspicious. Having the skills to mentally assess situations objectively is important. That way, there is no need to second-guess yourself, and you will grow in confidence regarding how you process people and situations. You are protecting yourself in the best way from danger, hurt and disappointment. Safety in all areas is your right; take it.

'Creating space for my welfare is one thing I will always take seriously. There is only one me, and I am loved and needed. My wellbeing is important to me and others; I will not take it lightly.'

Affirmation 117

There are so many negative emotions we have to fight through, some leaving us feeling guilty at times. Envy, jealousy, anger…whatever it is you may struggle with, take a moment and ask yourself what happened to put you in that place. You can find the answers to what is controlling you so you can be in control. Yes, you CAN be in control.

'I have the power to control and regulate my emotions once I recognise what they are. I will pay attention to why I have these emotions, and I will begin to address them so I can be free to live an emotionally balanced life.'

Affirmation 118

*L*ove can sometimes hurt, but love anyway. Sometimes, love can betray, but love anyway. Sometimes, love can let you down, but love anyway. When we shut off our heart because of the hurtful experiences we have gone through, we shut out the chance for real love to find its way in.

'I will open my heart to let out the darkness of pain, unforgiveness and bitterness. I will open my heart to the light of loving without limits.'

Affirmation 119

Success can be a tricky word to use because we compare ourselves to others. There are so many facets to us. Success may find us in our careers but not relationships or in our education but not in our other personal ambitions. So, you see, everyone has an area of growth, so allow yourself and others to grow and leave the comparisons alone. They'll only leave you feeling inadequate, and that is something you should never feel.

'I run my own race at my own pace. I will always remind myself that I am a success story unfolding.'

Affirmation 120

They say a person's home is their castle. A safe place. A fortress and a place to relax, be comfortable and content. Our environment plays such a crucial role in our mental and physical wellbeing. Be mindful of what and who you allow in your home. It really is your sanctuary, so guard it and make sure it's your happy space.

'I will create a space that allows me to breathe easy. I will create a space that allows me to think freely. My home is one of peace. Whether I live in a room or a mansion, I am my happy home.'

Affirmation 121

It can be really hard to keep calm when there is chaos all around you, but your surroundings don't mean your responses and mind have to be chaotic, too. Breathe slowly, count to ten and focus. Go to that calm place again, and put your thoughts together.

'I am not moved by the problems that I face and need to deal with. I do not react. I respond with calmness, wisdom, emotional intelligence and maturity. The solution will be found. I am patient in my pursuit of it.'

Affirmation 122

Hoping that things will get better is the first step. Without hope, we are guaranteed to be stuck. So, now that we agree on that, what are you going to do to make things better? What needs changing? The power to effect change is always in the hands of the one who needs it.

'I am more than able to put the necessary plans in place to bring about the changes that I need. I will not be a passive spectator in my own life. I will take control by putting actions to my words and desires.'

Affirmation 123

The world is full of beautiful people of all different shapes, colours, religions, ages and sizes. How sad to only venture where we know. Our blessings are hidden in all sorts of different packages, so start being on the lookout; you will be so surprised at what you will find in the unlikeliest of people.

'I am curious to find out more about the beauty I can find in all people. I will not allow my prejudice or fear to limit the many roads and avenues a higher power will use to bless me.'

Affirmation 124

Education isn't only learnt in the classroom. All around us, there is something new to experience every day. Be it from people, the things we go through, the things other people go through and share with us—each comes with it a valuable lesson on life waiting to be applied now or when we need it.

'I will open myself up to new experiences and opportunities daily. I will actively be on the lookout and listen out for what the world is trying to teach me. I am a good student who is ready to learn a little more than I knew yesterday.'

Affirmation 125

Our surroundings can tell a lot about where we are mentally. Usually, a lot of clutter and reluctance to let go of things because there is something we haven't dealt with or are internalising. It can be hard to let go of things we're attached to, but with help and support, taking one thing at a time, it will be possible, and the light can begin to break through the darkness.

'I will deal with the past and the things that will not let me let go so I can be happy in my now. I have the strength to open my palms and release things, so my open hands can receive the good and the new.'

Affirmation 126

Imagine walking along a beautiful sandy beach, listening to the waves and serenity of the moment. What if your circumstances are the opposite of this, and your situation reflects a picture of chaos? It can be hard to find peace or to create it if you've never known it, but that doesn't mean you don't deserve it. So, be bold, be brave, and call time on whatever is stealing your calm. You are definitely worth it.

'I don't have to live with chaos. I can have an existence of calm. I imagine a feeling of peace and calm. Carefreeness with no limits. I love the life I live.'

Affirmation 127

Joy comes in the morning. it truly does. After each dark day, a dawn breaks, signifying a new beginning you are a part of. Be joyful just for that blessing alone. Think of nothing else but the chance to create joy or find joy this new day.

'I am making a decision to bask in the moment. I am instructing my inner self to be joyful. I give my heart the command to be joyful this day.'

Affirmation 128

What is causing you to lose focus? What is taking you away from the things you want to achieve? There is so much vying for our attention. You only need to look away for a minute, and you lose track of time and focus. Keep your eye on the ball. Self-discipline may involve you saying 'NO' to yourself and getting rid of that distraction. DO IT!

'I will keep my focus and not be distracted. Whether it's a relationship, social media, a person—whatever is standing in the way of me achieving my purpose and my goals, I will do away with. All I see is the finish line. I will not go off track or be delayed.'

Affirmation 129

It's great to have great friends. True friends cheer you on and celebrate your achievements. True friends don't compete with you or are silent about your successes. If you have such a friend, redefine your understanding of friendship and hang around people who fit the new definition. Supportive, encouraging, kind–that is a true friend.

'I will always be mindful of who I share my success stories with. If I see or sense negativity or jealousy, I will pay attention and advise myself on what I want out of true friendship. I place a high value on me. I will not reduce the value of my friendship in the name of friendship. I deserve genuine cheerleaders in my camp.'

Affirmation 130

The best things in life are free, apparently, so why do they cost so much? Love and happiness can come at such a high price, but we must still pursue them if that is what we truly desire, and it's here that the price tag is attached. Love will cost you selflessness, putting others first and sacrificing, but the returns are great. Go ahead and invest.

'I am a magnet for good love and happiness. I have made my investments in myself and others, and I will reap the rewards. I will enjoy these things in my life.'

Affirmation 131

Hugs are said to help relieve stress, give us a sense of belonging and stability and makes us feel loved and secure. Wrap your arms around yourself and take deep breaths. Inhale and exhale. Tell yourself how special you are.

'I am wanted. I am needed. I create spaces of safety and love. I am calm and in control of all I need. As I breathe in and out, I exhale all my problems, all my fears. My breathing is calm and in sync with my heartbeat. I have regained my power to overcome stress and anxiety. I am calm.'

Affirmation 132

Sleep is so important to help us function mentally, physically and emotionally. When we are sleep-deprived, it can have such a profound effect on our wellbeing. Routine can help our sleep immensely, so turn off that TV. Play some calming music, have a bath or warm shower with scented candles in the room instead of regular light, close your eyes and think calming thoughts.

'I will prepare my evening and let go of the stresses of the day as the warm water washes over my body. I imagine the water washing away my cares, my fears and my anxieties. As I lay in my bed, my mind will rest as I think of peaceful thoughts.'

Affirmation 133

Gifts make us feel good because it tells us someone was thinking of us and makes us feel special. That feeling is beautiful and makes us feel loved and important, so pay it forward. Think of someone and give them a gift and say, 'Just because…' and see how you make them feel. Kindness always comes full circle.

'I will make someone feel special. I don't know what they might be going through. I will make it my mission to let someone know they are important, they are special, and they are worth it. I give love because I am love.'

Affirmation 134

Beware of wolves in sheep's clothing. Not everyone is how they appear to be. Some people wear many faces and many disguises, and it makes it hard to see who they are. Just hang around them long enough. The mask always slips, and you will see the face behind the mask.

'I will spend more time studying people before I lend them my trust. I will not just look at the surface of things. I will look much deeper before I expose my vulnerabilities. I am worthy of loyalty, true friendships and honest relationships.'

Affirmation 135

Water is healing. It hydrates, it replenishes, soothes and helps things grow. Water can also be so calming. How about going somewhere where you can feel the calming effects of water if you're feeling stressed? Everyone deserves that feeling of tranquillity, including you.

'I will take a walk by a lake, a walk in the rain or a stroll by the beach. I will speak out loud and hear my thoughts and still them. Peace is what I feel. I will meditate on this feeling and carry it with me when I need to lift the weight off my shoulders.'

Affirmation 136

When things fall apart and go wrong, it's hard to see the wood from the trees. A sense of helplessness and panic sets in because we feel out of control. We pray we stay in control, so we don't drop any of the many balls we often juggle. Truth is, even when things don't go to plan, it's all working together and will come good in the end. There is nothing to fear. Have a little faith.

'I cannot control what I can't see. I can only control what I feel. I choose to be at rest, and I choose to let go. I will stop trying to be God, needing to figure everything out on the spot. I will go with the flow and trust all things will work together for my good. I will rest easy.'

Affirmation 137

Don't ever let anyone steal your joy. You have the right to be joyful. Be intentional about those you let into your emotional space. If they make you feel miserable or unhappy about yourself, call time on them. When you find that happy space, protect it at all costs.

'I will protect my happy. I will not give anyone the power to dictate how I feel. I will ring-fence my heart and protect it at all costs. My joy is not up for debate.'

Affirmation 138

Paying compliments to complete strangers can change their whole day and how they perceive themselves. Tell somebody they look beautiful, that just seeing their smile has made your day, and see how you make theirs.

'I will be bold and fearless and speak to people I don't know. What's the worst that could happen? They may feel I'm a little crazy, but it would be a kind crazy, the kind of crazy the world needs, and the kind that I will give.'

Affirmation 139

Being alone isn't the same as being lonely. It's a great place to be when you can enjoy your own company and be left alone with your thoughts and not feel you're lacking anything. The most powerful place to be is where you can sit in contentment on your own. You are the best company you could ever have. Enjoy it.

'I appreciate the time I create to spend on my own because retreating into my zone is good for me. I am able to breathe, take stock and focus. My mental health is better for it.'

Affirmation 140

Trust is built; it's not something you can demand. If it's broken, it has to be earned. Have you broken someone's trust, or has someone broken yours? It's important to give those who are genuine the chance to earn that trust back. Extend that hand of grace as you would want it extended to you and rebuild that relationship. Nobody is perfect, but we all deserve a chance to make things right, including you.

'I will use my powers of wisdom and discernment to allow those with genuine hearts to earn back my trust. I will be clear and compassionate about what I need to ensure I am protected and heard in this process. I will have the final say on what is allowed in my emotional space.'

Affirmation 141

Everywhere we look, the not-so-nice things about life are there for us to see. Wars on television, poverty around the world and on our doorsteps. Life has been hard for many, and people in need surround us. What can we do to help the homeless person on the street? Help with food, clothes or even paying for a room for the night? Acts of kindness are life-changing. You have it in you to change someone's life, so do it.

'I will actively seek out those who I can be a blessing to. It is more blessed to give than to receive. It brings me joy to give of my heart, money, knowledge and time. I am a blessing to humanity.'

Affirmation 142

Don't let disappointment ruin your life. It's hard when you've had a deep longing for a dream to happen—like having children, getting married or enjoying a career—that never quite happened. Nobody should ever tell you not to dream or keep the faith, but if that dream hasn't happened yet, never let the wait or disappointment rule, define or break you. You are bigger than any dream.

'I will remember the dreams and the desires I have achieved. I will celebrate those daily and will always remember that I never failed at anything, but I did my best at trying. I have not failed just because I haven't got all the things I want. I am still a winner.'

Affirmation 143

Your word is your bond. When you promise something, mean it. When you say something, mean it. We are only as good as our word. Let's be mindful how we use them because we are judged by them the very moment they are spoken.

'I will speak with intention. My words will not be idle because my mind is not idle. I will keep my word and will stand by my word. I am a person of integrity.'

Affirmation 144

Life happens to all of us, but how we respond to the trials of life are different for everyone. Be mindful that your brokenness doesn't destroy others. Don't wound others because you are wounded. There is always a way to heal brokenness. Find it; it's waiting for you.

'My past will not control me. It will not ruin the people who have come into my life as a blessing. I will not punish those who did not cause my pain. I will set myself free, so I don't put anyone in bondage by knowing me. I will pursue freedom and enjoy life.'

Affirmation 145

A diamond is a diamond regardless of its carat, grade or size. Its value may differ, but its state doesn't. It's still a diamond, even when it's not been processed and covered in dirt. Don't ever see yourself as being less than just because a little dirt from life may be covering you. You are still valuable, and you are still a diamond.

'I will never see myself as less than. I will always remember my worth. I am just going through a process that I know, in time, will bring out the best in me. I am patient with me.'

Affirmation 146

The world is such a large place with so many people and places to see and explore. What's on your bucket list of things to do before you get married, or have children or get to a certain age? What's stopping you? If you haven't got a bucket list, write one! Goals are a great way of keeping you motivated and pushing for more out of life.

'I want to see more of the world and do things that have, up until now, just been dreams. I will create plans and timeframes to achieve my goals and celebrate each one as I achieve them. I will have no 'if only' moments in my life. I will get to do all that I set out to do.'

Affirmation 147

Never let shame force you into silence. Shame is not an emotion that you should feel. If you have been wronged, hurt, violated in any way, you have the right to use the power of your voice. Shame lies with the shameless, who hurt with no remorse, never with the one who is hurt. Lift your head high, push your shoulders back and walk tall. When you are ready, speak your truth.

'My voice is not to be silenced. Whenever I choose, at the right time for me, I will use my voice. Shame, embarrassment and fear are not mine. They do not belong to me. I do not want them. I hand them back to those who did wrong. I walk with no baggage from others. I am free.'

Affirmation 148

Breaking free from old habits that are bad for you can be hard; that's why they are called habits. Persistent harmful behaviours cannot always be stopped with willpower. Never feel embarrassed to speak with someone. Remember, it's silence that empowers the things that hold us hostage.

'I will not allow anything to have control over me. I will pursue what I need to take back my control. I will seek help from the right sources. I want to be better, and I will do better.'

Affirmation 149

What's that one big thing you thought you couldn't crack? How did you solve it? What approach did you use to change the outcome? You know what this proves? That you are smart enough to solve whatever comes your way. The next time that voice says you can't, whisper back, 'Watch me!' and go win again because that is what you are, a winner.

'If I fail at resolving an issue, I will try again. I have succeeded before, and I will succeed again. I will not give up. I will not take no for an answer. There is no problem I have that cannot be fixed.'

Affirmation 150

The sound of silence can sometimes be the most beautiful thing, but also it can be the most frightening. If you've lost a loved one, a relationship has ended, kids have left home, you've lost a pet—silence can really be painful. Don't feel silly if you have to speak out loud, it can really help you gain clarity on your thoughts. Speak and pour your heart out. Do it and feel better.

'I will do all I need to fill the void of loss. When I need to speak, I will speak and allow my heart to be emptied of whatever is causing me hurt and pain. My heart is for love and not sorrow. I will keep pouring out until I am okay.'

Affirmation 151

*L*ife has a funny way of pushing us into places that really bring out the best in us. We kick and scream and push against the things we assume aren't working in our favour, but the truth is, our obstacles are our stepping stones to success.

'I will stop assuming what doesn't go according to my plan means there isn't a better plan for me. A plan to guide me into where I need to be at the right place at the right time. All things work together and are designed to be a blessing to me.'

Affirmation 152

There is only one you. You cannot be all things to all people. You can't please everyone, even with the best intentions in the world. Do what you can without feeling pressured or resentful. Set your boundaries and respect them. Set the example for how others should treat you.

'I give of myself to help and support others but not at the expense of my wellbeing, happiness or values. I know I have a good heart. Saying 'no' does not make me a bad person. Those who appreciate me will understand me.'

Affirmation 153

Living peacefully with people will bring a sense of calm. You cannot control the actions of others, but you can control yours. Don't let others draw you into situations that make you lose control. Retain your power by keeping a hold of your emotions and your tongue.

'I will always pursue peace where I can. I will not let situations dictate my responses. I will let my standards guide me in times of conflict and confusion.'

Affirmation 154

Allowing people the grace to grow requires patience, maturity and honesty. How many silly things have we done in our time? We have to let others come into their own as we have come into ours. They are a work in progress, and so are we.

'I will not be judgmental of those on their journey. I am on mine. We are running the same race, arriving at the finishing line one at a time. As I extend grace, I open myself to receive grace.'

Affirmation 155

What do you do when you find yourself in a place where your worth is not recognised? Do you stay and try to prove them wrong beyond all reasonable doubt, or do you go to where you are celebrated? It's tempting to want to put the record straight, but for every second you spend trying to prove the naysayers wrong, you lose a second with people who could be rooting for you.

'My time and self-worth are valuable. I will never place opinions that don't matter above the knowledge I know of myself. I will always remember that I bring value wherever I go.'

Affirmation 156

Don't keep looking back. Allow the past to rest. If you keep looking back, you'll miss all the great things in front of you, and yes, they are great. All you need to do is change your position, and you will see clearly.

'I will make peace with the past so I can enjoy my future. I will let go of the hurt, the pain and the disappointment. I am ready to create the future I want because I am worth it.'

Affirmation 157

Life is a mystery that keeps unfolding. We can't always have all the answers before we step into the unknown. Sometimes, the unknown needs to remain hidden because if we could see what lay ahead, we may be too scared to take that leap into the bright future that awaits. Live limitlessly.

'I will take a leap of faith into the unknown. I will not try to control all the elements of my life. I trust that my life will go in the direction it needs to take me to my place of destiny.'

Affirmation 158

Things can happen to trigger anxiety, and it can be a tough thing to cope with. Anxiety only has a hold on you if you try to avoid what is causing the anxiety. Face the issue head-on. What is the worst that could happen? What is the solution to that worst-case scenario? The power of anxiety will have to loosen its hold once you tackle it head-on. You are greater than the anxiety.

'I will breathe. I will think calmly. I will look at the worst that could happen. I will not bury my head in the sand. I will be bold and face my fear head-on. I will look and find solutions to my problems. I am back in the driving seat. I am back in control.'

Affirmation 159

'A change is as good as a rest', so take the plunge and go look for that new job or start that business you've been thinking about. Whatever that change may be, go for it.

'I am ready to go for what I desire. I am able, and I am capable. I will put my heart and soul into what I want to do. My path to success has begun.'

Affirmation 160

Don't take yourself too seriously. Be silly once in a while. Let your hair down, and dance in the rain. Cherish those moments that put a smile on your face. We all need those moments that remind us that life is beautiful.

'I will never forget to take a moment to appreciate all the good things that life has to offer. No matter what is happening in this moment, I will savour it and appreciate it because I am here to enjoy it.'

Affirmation 161

Never be afraid to stand by your convictions. The fact that everybody is going in a certain direction doesn't mean you have to follow. Stay true to your beliefs. You do not need anybody's permission to have them.

'Even if it means standing alone, I will stand by my convictions. I trust my judgement enough to be the only one standing to defend them.'

Affirmation 162

In a room full of people, you can still feel so alone. The fake smile and forced laughter whilst you're dying inside—we've all been there. This is the one time you don't fake it till you make it; you'll break. Just stop for a minute and allow yourself to release the negativity. Nobody's watching. It's okay. Let it out.

'I don't have to pretend I'm okay. It's okay not to be okay. I will not set myself back by not being honest about how I feel. I know that nothing is resolved by burying my head in the sand. I will get my thoughts together so I can articulate how I feel and begin to find the solution to what is making me unhappy. I deserve happiness.'

Affirmation 163

It takes real confidence in who you are to celebrate those doing what you wish you could do. It takes a special kind of person to look on and appreciate the achievements of others. Well done; it says so much about you.

'I am happy to celebrate others. I am happy to see success in others. I am happy to see people live their best lives. My best life is loading. It is only a matter of time until I, too, am celebrated. Until then, I will cheer others on and genuinely be happy for them.'

Affirmation 164

Forgiving a wrong or an injustice can be one of the hardest things to do. Don't be afraid to forgive. No, it does not mean you have to still have a relationship with the person, nor does it mean you are weak. Forgiveness is not for the weak and cowardly; it's for the warrior in you.

'I am stronger than the pain. I am stronger than the hurt and disappointment. Yes, it may have had a huge impact on me, but I am now ready to make an impact on my life. I am focussing on being a better me. All other things no longer have my attention.'

Affirmation 165

When was the last time you treated yourself intentionally? Not the usual, spontaneous treats but planned treats of reward for all your hard work and how far you have come? If you can't remember ever celebrating yourself like that, then you'd better start. It's never too late to learn to pamper yourself just because…

'I will take out my calendar and mark a date and time to spoil me. I will write down my achievements over the last month. Number 1 will be successfully getting out of bed. It was hard, but I did it, and I faced the world anyway.'

Affirmation 166

Thank goodness so much is known about the impact of negative childhood experiences on adult life. Family life shapes, makes or breaks us, and it's amazing how much of home we carry into all aspects of our adult lives. If it's negative, and we're not aware of it, we just set up home with the same issues. We can change the status quo if we are willing to do the work and break the chains.

'I don't have to copy what I saw in my childhood. I can break the cycle of any behaviours that are unhealthy. I don't have to carry any negative legacies. I choose to be a bright new beginning for myself and my generation.'

Affirmation 167

Choose your battles wisely. Not everything needs to be honoured with a response. You know who you are. You have nothing to prove. Walking away from drama is not a weakness; it's an absolute strength.

'I reserve my strength for the wars that I really need to fight. I am selective of what I lend my energy to. I will not be coerced or goaded into battles that do not concern or benefit me. I will not be drawn into battle to be left wounded. If I fight, I fight to win.'

Affirmation 168

We are never at our best if our health is compromised. How do you do all that is expected of you if you're under the weather? Not very well, that's for sure! So, what can be done so the healing process can continue without interference? Rest is how. Rest allows your body to heal and your mind to rejuvenate. Relax; the world can manage without you while you put your health first.

'Taking breaks is necessary if I want to keep working at my best. I will not put anything above my health. I will treat my mind and body to treats like short holidays and rests as a normal thing I do for myself. I will not feel guilty by practising self-care or self-love.'

Affirmation 169

Music can truly soothe your soul. When we are sad, music can lift our spirits. It can express our feelings better than we can after a breakup. It can stop you in your tracks and just make you smile by bringing back those old memories. Music: it truly has the power to heal, so let it.

'I will set aside time to just listen to music and let the words and rhythm speak to my spirit and soul. I will enjoy the moment and allow my body and mind to relax and feel revived.'

Affirmation 170

Who upset you? Who robbed you of your joy? Who, when you remember them, ties your belly in knots and makes your blood boil? Don't give them another second. Take back your power by letting them go. Yes, it's hard. It doesn't mean they were justified in hurting you, or what they did to you was okay…but still, please, let them go so you can get YOU back. How long has it been? Take back the time you've given to this pain. Let peace reign.

'I am ready to release from my heart all those I have held there through bitterness and anger. I am releasing you (insert name of the person/persons who have wronged you). I am taking my power back. Revenge and bitterness no longer have a hold over me'

Affirmation 171

Who do you say you are? What do you use as the yardstick to measure yourself? This world will have you running all over the place, telling you about your looks, weight, financial power, what success looks like—it doesn't stop. So many voices telling you if you fit the definition of the world's 'perfect'. You define you. You tell the world who you are.

'I am me. I am anything I say I am. I am purpose. I am excellence. I am good health. I am sound mind. I am enough. That is who I am.'

Affirmation 172

If anyone told you change was easy, they lied! It may look easy, but it's tough. There are so many things you have to do outside your comfort zone that will stretch you, that will make you want to give up and settle, but don't. Just imagine achieving that change. Hold that thought for just a minute. The sense of pride and achievement. Meditate on that feeling. Visualise it in your mind's eye. Now, go out and change your world.

'I want and need to change and create change where I want to see things evolve. I will focus my mind on the end goal and respect the process. I know that through it all, I am learning lessons for life. I am not in a hurry. I will go at the pace the change dictates. I am ready.'

Affirmation 173

Value your supporting actors. We're all on a massive stage playing our assigned roles, but you're the main character in your play. Value those who help and support you to play your part well; you wouldn't look as good without them.

'I appreciate those who have helped me get to where I am. I am not self-made because I recognise the contributions of my friends and family and the experiences and opportunities that have created the "me" of today, and for that, I am truly grateful.'

Affirmation 174

They say when people show you who they are, believe them, but do we, or do we make excuses because we aren't ready to accept what we are being shown? It is never a good thing to make excuses for the poor or bad behaviour of others. Don't look on with your eyes wide shut. You are worth what you are convincing yourself you don't need: love, respect, compassion, understanding, support.

'I am worth all that I desire. I will make sure I am treated right by the ones I have invested in emotionally. It is no longer okay to be treated badly. I deserve to be treated more than well.'

Affirmation 175

There is no tax to pay on window shopping! Go out and look at those things you would like but maybe can't afford…at the moment. Go out and dream and come back and put a plan in place to make it happen. If you can dream it, you can have it. You just have to believe it.

'I dare to dream. I will challenge myself to go out and make my dreams a reality. I will keep pushing until something happens. Nothing is out of my reach.'

Affirmation 176

Don't be overwhelmed by the expectations of others. Set your own standards and start living. Don't be stifled by anybody's version of you. You'll never be able to meet them and remain happy, and you deserve to be happy with the original version of yourself.

'I am my own person. I am clear and certain of the person I want to be. I cannot be anything other than myself to the outside world. I will not attempt to please everyone. I will not make myself a candidate for insecurity by being less than honest with myself just to fit into the ideals of the outside world to feel accepted.'

Affirmation 177

It does not hurt to learn to keep your cards close to your chest at times. Not everything needs to be shared with the world before it manifests. The less people know of your plans, the less distraction and delay you will see in them coming to pass.

'I do not need an audience when I am working towards my goals or waiting for them to manifest. I will not be distracted by my need for reassurance from the outside world. Encouraging and spurring myself on is enough.'

Affirmation 178

People talk about voices in their head and all these thoughts doing what they want, creating havoc, but have you ever tried speaking aloud? Have you ever tried speaking aloud and having a conversation with yourself, where you can actually hear your own voice out loud, reasoning, complaining, encouraging? You will be surprised at how powerful the sound of your own voice is.

'I have a voice that is more powerful than I know. I will practice speaking aloud instead of letting thoughts run wild in my mind, holding me captive. I will speak out and dominate the voice in my head.'

Affirmation 179

All that glitters is not gold, so don't settle for what is not gold. Don't be dazzled by the shine. Substance is sustainable, so go for the long-term gain and genuine blessings. You deserve the best.

'I will not settle. I will work hard and work smart for what I want. I will not be swayed by what I see on the surface. I will exercise my powers of discernment and stay focused.'

Affirmation 180

*E*motions are important, and each one is to be respected. It is critical that we label emotions appropriately, so we know how to manage them. Don't look to pacify anger when what you feel is anxiety, which needs time to be analysed so you can address what is worrying you. Only then can you find the solution to what you are feeling.

'I embrace all my emotions. There is no right or wrong way to feel, but there is my way to feel, and it is valid. I do not have to justify my feelings or convince myself or others that I have the right to feel how I feel. My emotions are mine to own, embrace and express…respectfully.'

Affirmation 181

Not everybody is supposed to go the full distance with you.

Some people get on your bus for a fraction of the journey, some halfway, some right to the end…let them be. Don't stop them from getting off at their stop. You're not a kidnapper. Let them go. They've served their purpose.

'I will not hold anyone hostage. I will take the lessons my relationship and interactions with them have taught me. I will let them go. My peace will not be affected by their departure.'

Affirmation 182

There are going to be days when you feel less than. Days when you're tired, bored and fed up. Days where you pick yourself apart and can find nothing good to celebrate about yourself. STOP! Let's do something different today.

'Today, I choose to think about all the positive things about myself. I am a great person with a great mind. I am great. I don't need to ask the audience, I don't need to go 50/50, and I don't need to phone a friend. I am great, and that is my final answer.'

Affirmation 183

Most of us don't know when we are going to leave this earth. Although it may sound morbid, that's just a fact of life. What makes these conversations important is the fact that we don't want to leave this life with regrets. So, that person that you haven't told you love them even though you do, maybe today is a good day to let them know.

'I am purposeful with my words and my actions. I do not leave things to chance. I will consciously do the things that I need to do to live life without regret.'

Affirmation 184

When we have big assignments and tasks in front of us, the bigness of what we need to do can make us feel overwhelmed and worried, but we needn't be. Just like having a meal, we eat one morsel at a time, and before you know it, the meal is done. Why not take this approach when you're faced with something big? A piece at a time will get the job done. Don't sweat it.

'Nothing overwhelms me. Nothing intimidates me. Nothing will overcome me. Little by little, I will gain ground. Little by little, I am making headway. So long as I am moving, that is all that matters.'

Affirmation 185

Patience, indeed, is a virtue, but sometimes, our patience is stretched and tested. It doesn't take much to react to the first sign of offence or a situation that makes us uncomfortable. But if you take a deep breath and count to ten before you respond, you will find that your responses are far better thought out and unlikely to leave you with regret for what you wish you hadn't done or said.

'I have control over my words and my actions. I have control over how I wish to present myself. I do not allow things or people to determine how I express myself in unpleasant situations.'

Affirmation 186

When we speak of compatibility, we often refer to relationships, but have you ever thought about it in relation to your work? Are you compatible with the job that you have chosen? Are you compatible with the career path you've decided to take? How are you showing up, and how do you feel at the end of each day? Think about it, and you decide.

'I will not make do just because I have been in the same place for years or because I feel that I have made too much of an investment to walk away. If I'm not compatible with what I spend most of my time on, then I will not be afraid to make that change where compatibility and fulfilment become my friend.'

Affirmation 187

When we are hurt, it's really easy to play the blame game. We do that because we feel attacked and go into self-preservation mode. We look for a way of escape really to tend to our wounds. That's okay. Just try a little harder to be empathetic and see things through the eyes of the other person, who may also be hurting. The key isn't in proving who is right; the key is finding a solution for peace or a peaceful reconciliation.

'I have flaws, and I will not hide behind them. I am humble enough to admit when I am wrong, take ownership and put things right where I can. I do all I can do to preserve the relationships that are dear to my heart.'

Affirmation 188

Let's check in… how are you doing today? I mean, really, really doing today? Great? Not so great? Don't worry. If you're not doing too good today, remember when you had a tough time and got through it. You are still the strong, resilient, I-won't-give-up individual today that you were then. All that has changed is that you have more experience at winning.

'I won't run for the hills because of today's challenges. I have gotten through worse; I will get through this. I am a warrior.'

Affirmation 189

Sometimes, we come so far it's a shock to us, and we have to stop, look back and take it all in. Did that really happen? Did I really do that? Did I really come this far? The answer is 'Yes!' Yes, you did that. Yes, you came this far. Keep going because you will reach that finish line.

'I will keep going. I have what it takes to get to that finish line. I can see it. Every step I take, I get that bit closer. My eyes are fixed on the goal. I am making progress. I'm digging deep. Victory is in sight.'

Affirmation 190

The friends that come into our lives come to make, break or shake us. Nobody comes to us without us learning something from the experience. If we miss the lesson, we go through that class again until we pass that exam. Friends can be the greatest blessing or the greatest curse, but the most important thing is how we respond. What does the experience bring out in us? Always remember: you are worthy of love and loyalty.

'I have no control over how others do friendship, but I have complete control over the kind of friend I am. I trust myself to be dependable, honest and compassionate. I trust myself to have clear boundaries and not feel guilty if I have to remind others of them or walk away if my boundaries are not being respected.'

Affirmation 191

It's okay to excel or want to do well. You don't have to pretend you're not great just to make others feel comfortable in your presence. You cannot shrink yourself in favour of pretending to be average, so you're easier to be around.

'I am proud of who I am. I am not perfect, but I am happy with where I am. I will not apologise for doing well. I am not in competition with anyone. I am not responsible for the insecurity of those who come into contact with me.'

Affirmation 192

*B*e prepared for your future. Don't be caught off guard by not being intentional with your time. Time has a funny way of creeping up on you and showing you all the opportunities you missed. Don't put off today what you can do today. Regret is an enemy of your peace and happiness.

'Failure and regret are not my portion. I put my hopes and dreams into a tangible action plan and execute my plans with intention and passion.'

Affirmation 193

Mind what you watch; watch what you listen to. Poor choices in either one will seep into your soul. It takes more than wishful thinking to put you in a space where your thoughts and emotions are healthy. If you watch and listen to programs and music that promote fear and negative thoughts, you will be negative and fearful. Pour into you what you want to pour out of you.

'I am responsible for my wellbeing. I will not fill my mind with things that contaminate my thinking and upset my emotional wellbeing. I will watch and listen to things that uplift and edify my soul.'

Affirmation 194

'Show your haters that you made it.' How many times have we heard this? Truth is, if you're worried or concentrating on your haters, then you're distracted. You will lose focus if you're looking at anyone but yourself. You are the only one who deserves your attention. Focus.

'I am the only one I have my eyes on. My progress is for me to achieve and enjoy. I will not give people who do not have my best interest at heart my time. I work on my goals for myself, not to prove anyone wrong, but to prove myself right.'

Affirmation 195

What is the true price of your loyalty? How easy would it be for you to lower your values and moral standards? Have you ever compromised what you believe in because it benefited you to do so? No judgement, just an opportunity for you to question who you really are.

'I am a work in progress. I know my integrity will be tested. I will do my best not to crack under pressure. My heart is on the side of what is right. That is where I am; that is where I wish to remain.'

Affirmation 196

Your mind is a power tool, so don't let it work against you. Treat it like the precious thing that it is. Stimulate it, empty it of bad thoughts, fill it with dreams. Your mind is your best friend. Treat it with respect.

'I will treat my mind as a valuable safety deposit box. I will only deposit what is valuable. I hold the key to what I deposit. I will keep the combination secret, and I will guard that key passionately.'

Affirmation 197

Rise and shine half an hour earlier in the morning. Go for a walk. Take in the fresh air and appreciate nature and the absolute wonder that it is, then look in the mirror and be in awe of the greatest wonder of them all.

'I will never get tired of saying I am fearfully and wonderfully made. I am special. I am unique. I am amazing. The world is blessed and better because I am in it.'

Affirmation 198

Raise your hands and just give thanks. Be thankful for your children, your job, your cat, your dog, your loved ones, the car that started, the train you just caught, that letter you've been waiting for. Be thankful; it attracts more things to be thankful for.

'I am thankful for all that I have. I take nothing for granted. I may not have everything I want, but I am grateful for what I have. May my heart always be one of thanks and gratitude.'

Affirmation 199

A good attitude can take you anywhere you need to go in life. It can open doors for you, it can cause perfect strangers to come to your aid and to your defence. Your attitude can literally change a decision that could have gone against you in your favour. Don't ever lose this kind of attitude; you never know who is watching.

'I choose to show up with an attitude that draws goodness and blessings to me. I am consciously exhibiting to others the kind of attitude I would like to experience from them.'

Affirmation 200

Find something you love doing; that's the only way you will do it with excellence. Don't stay in a job or career that doesn't make you want to jump out of bed in the morning or waste years of study on something you're not passionate about. Your life is way too important not to ignite that fire in you.

'I will not make do because it's easy. I will find my passion in what my heart truly desires. I will enjoy what I do and make sure it gives me joy and a purpose that keeps me motivated.'

Affirmation 201

We are often told to not be angry, but not this time. Be angry. Be in control of the emotion that is a valid and correct response to what has happened to you. Be honest about how you feel instead of being in denial. You will feel resentful and run the risk of seething with anger if you downplay how you really feel, and that is not healthy. Acknowledge it, process it and deal with it. Now, put it to rest and move forward.

'I understand the emotions I feel. I am in control of them, and I will not invalidate them. I will process my anger, pain and disappointment. I will not disempower myself by remaining angry. I will let this emotion flow through me and find its place of rest outside of me.'

Affirmation 202

The only way to overcome fear is to confront it. What is causing you to fear? What makes you retreat into yourself? Don't you know who you are? Don't you know you are great? You don't have to feel great as proof! You just are.

'I am bold. I will confront my fears straight on and move through them. No thing has the right to cause me to fear.'

Affirmation 203

Love is not just a feeling; it's a choice. It takes a lot to decide to love the 'unloveable'. The funny thing is we don't realise that we are the 'unloveable', yet we still want and need love in our ugliest moments. Think about that the next time you want to give up on someone who needs you to see beyond their imperfections.

'I will learn to be as patient and as compassionate as I wish others would be to me. I will extend a hand of love and friendship to those who need it the most but receive it the least. I will be a bridge of hope.'

Affirmation 204

Iron sharpens iron. Be around people who push and challenge you to be better in a healthy and balanced way. Seek out people who will push you to do better.

'I will not allow fear or insecurity to draw me to people who do not bring out the best in me. I will not be afraid to be around those who have achieved what I desire. I will be inspired by them so I can do better.'

Affirmation 205

*G*ood and true friends are hard to come by. If you can find one who has your best interest at heart, hold them dear. Find a friend who will keep and hold you accountable, who continually challenges you to be better.

'I will appreciate those who have been planted in my life and along my path to keep me accountable and to make me a better person. I appreciate my true friends, and I will be there for them as they have been there for me.'

Affirmation 206

What motivates you? What spurs you on? What is it that gives you a reason to not give up and keep going? Hold on to that thing, that reason, that person, and let it continue to inspire you and push you.

'I am focused. I am determined to reach my destination of achievement. I will not be distracted nor discouraged. I am keeping my eye firmly on the ball, no matter what is going on around me.'

Affirmation 207

Reject invitations to pity parties. There is no good music, the food sucks and the people are boring. Trust me: there is nobody worth meeting at these parties. Politely decline the invite and opt for a quiet night in. And if, by any chance, you're throwing this party, call it off. You don't need to be there.

'I will not allow my circumstances to make me feel that I have to be the walking wounded. For a little while, I will respect the emotion I am feeling, but I will move on and look for the solution to what is making me feel down, and I will find it.'

Affirmation 208

*Y*ou are not a chameleon. You are you, and you are enough. You do not ever have to change who you are to fit in. The beautiful colours that make you you are just right for the environment you're in. Don't ever change the colours of your character to fit a picture that you are not meant to be in.

'I have a personality and character that fits perfectly for where I am supposed to fit. I am okay as I am. I don't EVER have to change who I am to be appreciated, loved or accepted by people who matter. If I am not appreciated, loved or accepted, then they don't matter—I do.'

Affirmation 209

Whatever is placed in you as your gift is placed in you for the world to see and for the world to benefit. You are born for service. Share what you have for the love of others. What you have in you is not just for you—it is also for the people.

'I am willing to look for where I can share my gift with others. If it's to be a listening ear, helping those less fortunate than myself, or supporting someone, I am willing and able. I understand I am a gift to others.'

Affirmation 210

There is enough of the pie to go round. You don't need to be envious and jealous of others. There is no need to take that which is not yours. No need to lie and cheat to gain what is not meant for you.

'I am content to enjoy what's mine. My achievements have been through honesty and hard work. I do not need to step on or over others to get to where my ambitions are calling me.'

Affirmation 211

Don't wait for payback to happen; it's a distraction to your progress. When people do you wrong, just leave them be. Don't waste your time trying to make them see the error of their ways. They will see it, I assure you. You focus on the lessons you learnt from what they did and stay focused.

'I will travel with no emotional baggage filled with hate, revenge or unforgiveness. I will empty myself of all negative emotions from those who have hurt me. I will busy myself with healing and being whole.'

Affirmation 212

Don't clock-watch. Keeping time is a distraction that robs you of your now. Don't make yourself anxious because you haven't quite learnt that patience is really a virtue and a formidable character trait. You will be much more relaxed and at ease when you learn to be patient.

'Patience is a virtue and one I possess. I understand that I will be put in situations where my patience will be tested. I choose to keep being tested until I pass with flying colours.'

Affirmation 213

Every so often, take the time to take in nature and reconnect with the things you see around you. Appreciate the birds, the clouds, the air you breathe and the very essence of life. Once in a while, it's good to revisit the uncomplicated things in life. It promotes gratitude and appreciation; that is never a bad thing.

'I will always find a moment to be still and appreciate the things I can see, feel, smell, touch and hear. I am blessed to be in this moment. I am grateful to experience life.'

Affirmation 214

Joy brings strength, and sadness makes you weak. When you are joyful, it brings you a measure of strength that is the fuel to your fire. Notice how, on the other hand, when you're sad, how drained and lethargic you can feel. In those moments, look for the little things that bring you joy and start to find the strength that you need to get through such times.

'This feeling will pass soon. I will not always feel sad or down. I will be conscious about my highs and lows, and I will take note of what makes me feel down. I will be proactive in managing my thoughts and emotions as best as I can.'

Affirmation 215

Be honest, plain and consistent. Don't have a double tongue; nobody trusts a person who says one thing one minute and another the next. When people know where they stand with you, they stand with you.

'I am honest. I have integrity. I stand for what is right. I am not swayed to say what the masses are saying. I will be consistent and fair with my words. I have the confidence to speak truth no matter who I have in front of me.'

Affirmation 216

Don't blame your failures on anyone. See them as necessary lessons you need to learn for your life's journey. Your perception of your situation will determine whether it makes or breaks you. Don't let a defeatist and negative mindset keep you feeling sorry for yourself.

'I will do what it takes to succeed at the things I have lost. I will make a conscious effort to look inside myself and look at where I can do and be better. I will take ownership of the things I say and do. I will strive to be a better me.'

Affirmation 217

What it is you desire? Invest in someone who has what you want. Seeds bear fruit. Sow into the lives and dreams of others in the areas you want to excel and see what happens.

'I am an investor in the dreams of others. I will help others get to where they wish to go, and I will celebrate those who are where I hope to be. I am a cheerleader, and I enjoy seeing the accomplishments of others.'

Affirmation 218

Always be well-prepared and focused. When opportunity comes, you will be ready to step into what you have been waiting for. You will step in with confidence, knowing you have earned your place through your hard work, commitment and dedication.

'I am getting ready for the opportunities that I know are coming my way. I will not be idle, waiting for my desires to fall into my lap. I am working with passion, consistency and tenacity to prepare myself for the opportunities when they present themselves.'

Affirmation 219

You are an onion! There are so many layers to you, some you have yet to discover yourself. So, let me ask: why the one-dimensional perspective of yourself? Why the tunnel vision and assessment of your value and capabilities? If this layer of where you are in life is making your eyes water, keep peeling, and with time, self-love and self-discovery, you will find the goodness and value you are looking for.

'I am still finding out about myself. Life is a journey, and I am on a journey of self-discovery. This journey is never-ending as I grow in wisdom, age and experience. I will keep evolving. I will keep embracing the new me.'

Affirmation 220

Don't be discouraged because things don't seem to be going your way. Keep your chin up and keep the faith. Life is like that sometimes, topsy-turvy and jumbled up. In time, things will sort themselves out, just trust the process.

'I will not worry about the things I don't understand or things I don't have an answer to. I won't let anything get me down. With calm anticipation, I know things will get better.'

Affirmation 221

People are all right with you being all right, but not all right with you being great. It's just one of life's miseries…or is that mysteries? Not everyone will celebrate you winning. It's okay. Keep going and be your best anyway. The real ones will cheer you on.

'I will not be upset or disappointed by the darker side of human nature. I will go where there are like-minded people who are not intimidated by my success.'

Affirmation 222

Don't be afraid to let people pour into you once in a while. Nobody was designed to keep giving beyond their capacity. Take time out to recharge your batteries. You are important too. You are needed.

'I am ready and willing to ask and receive help when I need it. If I am tired, I will say. When I am afraid, I will say. When I need help, I will say. I will rest and replenish myself. I will make sure I operate from a place of fulness and not deficit.'

Affirmation 223

Being in touch with your emotions is a wonderful thing, but don't allow your emotions to be used against you. Emotional blackmail is damaging, and you don't want to get to a place where your experiences harden you. Keep that beautiful and compassionate nature you have.

'I will be wise in whom I allow to benefit from the compassion I show, but I will not allow my good nature to be used against me. I will not be made to feel guilty because I don't want to do something. It is my choice to do whatever I am being asked.'

Affirmation 224

What words are you speaking over yourself and your situation? If your words speak defeat, then that is what will happen. If your words speak victory, that is what you will have. Decide on the outcome you are looking for and speak it into existence.

'I am not double-minded. I am clear about my expectations and the outcomes I want. I speak positive things into the atmosphere, so I expect positive results from the words I speak, and the faith I place behind my words.'

Affirmation 225

Old habits die hard, but they can die. Be determined to kill what does not benefit you. If you can learn to do something, you can unlearn it. How much do you want to be free?

'I will be strong and not weak. I will find the strength and support to unlearn the things that hurt me and others. I want to be free from all the things that do not serve a positive purpose in my life.'

Affirmation 226

Laugh at yourself once in a while, and don't take yourself so seriously; life is serious enough as it is. Let loose and let go; it'll do your sanity a great favour and give it a break from being sensible all the time. We all have a little crazy in us; you are not alone.

'I am not afraid to relax and be myself without worrying about who is looking or what others think. I am not perfect, but there is no such thing. There is me, perfectly imperfect in all my ways. I am wonderful, even in my mad moments.'

Affirmation 227

Don't bring your past into your future. Some things have served their purpose. Allow those things to rest. Embrace the future, even if you don't know what the future holds. Believe your future is better than your past. Be expectant.

'I have made peace with the things that have happened in the past. Some things I understand, others I don't. I am okay knowing I have a lifetime to enjoy what lies ahead of me, starting today.'

Affirmation 228

Revenge is a dish best served cold, apparently, but you'll be the one slaving to put that dish together. You can spend your time, effort and sweat to ensure you pay back what was done to you, or you can choose to release those who have offended you and create your happy.

'I will give no one the power to make my heart vengeful. I will not give my emotional power to anyone through my desire for revenge. I will go on with my life, and life will take care of the rest.'

Affirmation 229

Don't apologise for the life experiences you have had. Don't be ashamed of the things you did to survive. The war is over. You can exhale and rest and be proud of who you are today.

'I am not ashamed of my past. I look back and see how much I have grown and how far I have come. I am proud that I have overcome the things many would not be able to handle. I am not ashamed of the things that have shaped this awesome human being called 'me'.

Affirmation 230

Don't let anything stop you from being who you want to be. If you want that new body, go for it. If you want that new job, go for it. If you want to get healthy, go for it. Let no one put limitations on you. You are your own starting and finishing line.

'I am determined and focused on the change I want to see. I am keeping my vision locked onto what I want to be. Only I have the combination to unlock it. I hold the key to my change. I will not give up for anything.'

Affirmation 231

We all have challenges in being able to achieve the things we desire. Each and every one of us. Don't let anyone tell you you're a failure and don't you ever believe it. The one thing they don't know is how your story will end.

'I am not a failure. I am an unfolding story with a happy and good ending. I will not give any weight to the words of those who do not hold my future in their hands.'

Affirmation 232

Do you start tasks and leave them lingering, always with the intention of completing them, but don't? You would be surprised at what that can tell you about yourself. It takes a lot of organisation and self-discipline to finish what you start. It is a trait that will serve you well in all areas of your life.

'I commit to finishing what I start. I will think through what I want to achieve and let that be one of the things that motivate me to complete what I put my hand to. I will not leave any part of my life unfinished. I am dedicated to all tasks that I own.'

Affirmation 233

A lack of self-confidence can show up in many ways, and one of them is trying to keep up with the Joneses. Don't feel the need to live like anyone else. Live within your means, and if that is not enough, work towards something that will let you live the life you've dreamed of.

'I will not settle, but I am content with what I have. I will not let envy into my heart or my mind because I want what others have. I will not be distracted. I will be intentional and have a plan to get the things that are meant for me.'

Affirmation 234

Accept people for who they are. If you've chosen to love or befriend them in the state that you found them, then do that. Don't try and force them to be the version you want. Change has to be a person's choice, just like how you need to decide if and when change is necessary for you.

'If I choose to love people as I find them, I will not manipulate them into change. I will love and accept as I find. If they need to grow, I will grow alongside them. I will make sure my connections are harmonious and supportive.'

Affirmation 235

Plan A or Plan B? That is the question! Do you only have a plan A because there's no option to fail? That isn't necessarily a bad thing. Or are you a plan B person? If A doesn't work, you have something to fall back on. What's important is whatever your method to success, you keep forcing those doors to open and not give up.

'I am committed to the vision I have for my life. I will not stop going until what I have set my heart on manifests. I will not allow any curveballs to throw me off course. I will keep going.'

Affirmation 236

When things have not gone your way during the day, and people have upset you, try not to go to bed angry. One thing that is guaranteed is that thing will play on your mind and most likely affect another day. Don't let the sun go down on your anger. Rather, let peace rise with you in the morning.

'I will release and let go of all the negativity of the day. I will put to rest the things that have upset my spirit. I will take control of my tomorrow. I will go to bed peacefully, and I will rise peacefully.'

Affirmation 237

Say 'I love you' to the ones you love often. Be it to your children, your spouse, your partner, siblings, parents, friends… say it often. Nobody gets tired of those words when spoken with a genuine heart and when needed.

'I will not take for granted the time I have with the ones I love. I will express my love often and never leave things unsaid.'

Affirmation 238

Needing help does not mean you're weak; it means you're human. There's no rulebook that says you have to do it all alone or figure it out all by yourself. You only need to ask and share the load.

'I am not afraid or too proud to ask for help. Strength is for the strong, and help is for those who need help. I will attract all I need to help me when I need it. I will seek help, and I will humbly accept help because strong people need help, too.'

Affirmation 239

The art of resolving conflict requires patience, tact, maturity and skill. The true spirit behind resolving conflict is not to prove who is right or who is wrong but rather what will bring peace between people.

'I will not use my influence to bring division. I will use my influence as a positive force to bring people together. I am honest, and I have integrity. I will know what to say at the right time to restore peace to those who need it. I am a facilitator of peace.'

Affirmation 240

What do you do when you don't fit in? Do you recoil and find a place to be as inconspicuous as possible? Do you find a corner to sit in and hope the time passes quickly so you can go home and hide? Did it ever occur to you that you aren't supposed to fit in, and it's an opportunity for you to appreciate how beautiful it is to be different?

'I do not apologise for my uniqueness and my quirkiness. I was not made to fit in; I was made to stand out in all the right places. I am confident in the skin I am in. I am confident in being me in any situation at any time and in any place.'

Affirmation 241

A broken relationship can sometimes spell a broken you. Putting yourself back together again is no mean feat. It'll take time. There'll be days when you feel like you're drowning…relax, but only so you can float on the water. Close your eyes and breathe. The pain will pass, and you will get stronger.

'My relationship may be broken, but I am not broken. I am reforming to be a better me. I may feel down, but it will pass. I will hold onto the good memories and let go of those that bring me pain. I am evolving into a stronger, healed me.'

Affirmation 242

Are you a good friend? We are quick to judge the horrid experiences we have had with friends, but are we different? Being a good friend requires a lot, and we will always be tried and tested to see if we measure up. If it's important to us, we will always be a person who will be a friend that is there for the long haul.

'I am the best friend anyone could have. I am a friend who loves sincerely. I am dependable and loyal. I do not take advantage of my friends. I love and value those I call friends because I love and value myself.'

Affirmation 243

Do life at your own pace. Only you know the internal battles you're facing and how much it takes to get through the morning to the evening. Take each hour, not day, at a time. Sometimes, the thought of getting through a whole day is too daunting. Pat yourself on the back for each hour you get through.

'I will take my time and get through each moment by breathing. I will think calm thoughts and commend myself each hour I get through. I will be better. I am better. I will be more than okay.'

Affirmation 244

When nobody is watching, who are you? Are you one person in front of an audience and another when you're alone? Being two people when you're one person is a hard act to keep up. Decide who you want to be and be that person.

'I am consistent, and I am honest. I am open, and I am transparent. I am a safe person to be around. What you see is what you get. I am an open book. Integrity is my name.'

Affirmation 245

When you have gone through a lot of rejection in your life, it's hard to love yourself. After all, how can everyone be wrong? Well, they can be. Learn to like yourself, and soon, that like will turn to love, and the rejection of others won't matter so much.

'I have accepted myself. I am a person of exceptionally high value. It is okay if others do not see it. I see it, and that is all that matters.'

Affirmation 246

Love your own company enough not to always need to have people around you. When you love chilling with you and being with you, you never fear being on your own. You never fear being alone because you never are.

'I don't need other people to make me feel content. I don't rely on company to make me feel I belong. I am okay being with me. I am a safe, fun and great place to be.'

Affirmation 247

We all have someone we've aspired to be like at some point in our lives, and that's a good thing. It means we recognise in someone else something we would like to emulate. After admiring those traits, what next? The work begins. Whatever you admire that has caught your eye requires some work, so roll up your sleeves and start working on you.

'I will dig deep and do what it takes to transform myself into the person I desire. I will be who I design and work on myself to be. I am a work in progress, and I am progressing.'

Affirmation 248

When was the last time you really laughed? That bellyaching, floor-rolling, struggling-to-breathe laugh? It's a beautiful thing, isn't it? Recalling those memories will do wonders in those moments when you're left alone with your thoughts.

'I will create moments that bring me and others joy. I will cherish the memories I create and recall them in my dark moments. I will place these times in my heart and cherish them.'

Affirmation 249

In order to cope with certain situations, we need to learn to emotionally regulate ourselves. We may need to count to ten, or breathe slowly, maybe even take ourselves outside for a walk to cool down. Being able to regulate your feelings is safer for you and those around you. Don't feel guilty for stepping away from an impending explosion.

'I will exercise self-control and be in control of my actions. Nobody holds a remote control over my feelings or my actions. I am a conscientious and emotionally balanced individual, able to articulate my feelings no matter the situation. I will show up as I wish and not how circumstances force me to be.'

Affirmation 250

You can't please all the people all the time, but be mindful of how you treat those you inevitably may disappoint. Try to be empathetic in your dealings with others. You will be glad you did if your paths cross later in life.

'I take nobody for granted. No one is insignificant in my walk of life. I appreciate and respect everyone who has crossed my path. I appreciate all who have contributed to my life. For good or for bad, I embrace all who have taught me the lessons I need for my journey.'

Affirmation 251

Don't ever be afraid of growing old. It can be scary because your body is changing, you haven't achieved all you want out of life, and you don't know if you will. Nobody can tell you about tomorrow, but you have today. Live in the now and just enjoy the things within your reach in this moment.

'Accepting change is part of life. I am blessed to be a part of change. I am blessed to witness change. I am not afraid of tomorrow. I welcome my future with open arms. I welcome the experiences I am having now.'

Affirmation 252

No man is an island. 'You Might Need Somebody', in the famous words of soul singer Randy Crawford, so don't cut yourself off from people. Be there for others and put yourself out once in a while. We have all needed, will need and are going to need somebody at some point in our lives, and if we don't, somebody will need us.

'I will lend myself to others because I have a heart that enjoys giving. I know I am the answer to someone's need. I know that I will have an answer to my needs from the right person at the right time. I will never be too proud to ask for help. I have invested enough in others to not feel guilty for wanting to reap a harvest when I need to.'

Affirmation 253

If ever you feel you're drowning, come up for air. Wave your hands. The lifeguards will see you. They'll either swim out to you or hand you a life jacket. You're never going to be left alone; somebody will always swim out to help you.

'I will not suffer in silence. There is always someone waiting to attend to my cry. I will stop and take stock in times when I have so much on my plate I don't know what to do. I will take my time to swim through whatever troubled waters I find myself in. Dry land is in sight. I will be fine.'

Affirmation 254

Watch what you use to define who you are. If it's looks, money, your career or marital status, just be mindful when and if those things change or you lose them, you're not left feeling lost, naked or without an identity. You have always and will always be more than a status, no matter how great it is.

'Nothing defines me. Nothing that can be lost or taken away gives me my identity. My identity is internal and shines on the outside. I will not be placed in a labelled box. I am more than an identity determined by things. I am me, all by myself.'

Affirmation 255

What values do you hold dear? If you want to be in a relationship or cultivate relationships that are healthy, make sure your values align. It's when issues show up that will determine how you respond to your conflicts and disagreements that you'll wish you had something more than attraction or interests in common.

'I will look beyond the surface of those I choose to love to determine real connections and values. Because I am of high value, I will not devalue myself by placing the wrong things above the truth of what I see.'

Affirmation 256

Be your greatest advocate. Plead your own cause. In doing so, you will know where you've made mistakes. You will know what you need to correct. The beauty is you can do that without prying eyes and the judgement of others. The privacy to grow at your own pace, at your own rate, with no pressure.

'I will go through a systematic and clear thought process of where I am right and where I may be wrong. I will look at what I need to do differently and do it. No excuses. I will take responsibility and do what it takes to show up how I want.'

Affirmation 257

You are amazing. No question, no doubt, no argument. Sometimes, you just have to forget about your flaws and give yourself a boost! That's it! That's all that's required today! You are amazing! End of story…

'I am amazing. No argument. No second-guessing. No talking myself out it or dumbing down that I am…amazing. Every drop of me. Yes, I have said it, and I believe it.'

Affirmation 258

Leave the pain of your story where it is. Going back to a place that puts you in emotional pain is not healthy. Let the memories rest so you can rest. It's okay to be happy. Give yourself a break. Give yourself a break from the past.

'I am not my past. I may never have all the answers. I may ask, 'Why me?' but it's okay that it was me. I am here to tell the tale of when I overcame. I don't have to tell the story from when I was on the ground anymore. I rose, and still, I rise.'

Affirmation 259

What we term as being of value can be subjective. The key is to not let anyone tell you what you feel is valuable isn't so, just because it means nothing to them. Hold the things you love close to you, and don't let anyone devalue what is important to you.

'I have no need to justify what I choose to hold dear. If it's to play golf on the weekends or go let my hair down with a few friends, whatever I need that gives me the feel-good factor and does not harm me or others, I give myself permission to enjoy those things because I am worth it.'

Affirmation 260

Don't leave people wounded by their association or interaction with you. Be mindful of how you speak to people and how you treat them. Not everyone has the confidence to say you hurt their feelings. Don't allow anyone to carry internal pain because of you.

'My intentions are not to wound but to heal. I will continue to be a shelter for those who are wounded. I will ease the pain of others. I will consciously and deliberately be a source of healing and peace for those who connect with me. I will leave people blessed by my presence.'

Affirmation 261

Nobody can ever love you more than you. If you're struggling to be the love of your life, others will struggle, too. You have to demonstrate how you want to be loved by loving on you. Set the example you need others to follow.

'I am learning to love me. I am lovable. I will not believe what others have said or done to me in this area of my life. A parent, a friend, a partner—it does not matter. I have the final say. I am worthy of love. I choose to love myself. I set the foundation for others to follow. I love me.'

Affirmation 262

Nobody in this world is irrelevant or insignificant. We are all part of the same body, functioning in the part of the body that we're placed. The hand is no less important than the heart. If you need to cover your heart from an arrow aimed at it, you'll see its value. We're all important and special; the right time will show you how much.

'I recognise and appreciate the value we each play in the lives of one another. Nobody is small; nobody is insignificant. I am not small. I am not insignificant.'

Affirmation 263

What's that one thing you wished you'd done or want to do? What's that thing that gives you that little hint of regret or sadness? Not because it didn't work out but because you've never tried. Fear of failure? That's the best fear to have. It means you care, and that's a great starting point… so start! Dare to dream, but dare to make that dream a reality.

'My road to success may involve some failures. That means I have one less method to try, but I am going to try. I will not give up. I will not allow fear or pride to stop me. I will seek help, and I will accept help, and if I fall, I will get up and try again. Giving up on my dream is not an option.'

Affirmation 264

Don't ever put your confidence and trust in another human being to the point where their failures can devastate you. We are all human, and humans make mistakes, and humans fail. Don't place 100% responsibility on somebody being perfect when we haven't reached that level of excellence ourselves.

'I will not burden anyone to live up to an unrealistic expectation of being perfect. I will be gracious to myself and others and allow them the luxury of making mistakes. I will be fair to those I have in my camp and to myself. I will allow myself to grow and others to grow, too.'

Affirmation 265

Pace yourself if you don't want to run out of steam. Creating a realistic pace at which to work will allow you to take stock, plan and execute your vision without pressure. Pressure creates desperation; desperation leads to mistakes; mistakes lead to regret.

'I will have a plan in place that considers my mental and emotional wellbeing. I will not chase a dream that leaves me too emotionally and mentally unfit to enjoy it. I am balanced in all I do, and I take care of me no matter what I set out to achieve. I do this because I am worth it.'

Affirmation 266

If you're worried about something and it's overwhelming, who can you speak to? Don't keep it locked up. Worry can truly make you sick. Share the load, even if it's to a perfect stranger; it may help. If you don't have anyone, take a walk and speak to the wind. Speaking your words outside of yourself can bring relief. I pray you find relief and rest from whatever is troubling you.

'I know I will find help if I seek it. Whatever is troubling me can be solved. I look outside of myself for solutions. I have the faith to believe that things will get better. I rest my mind and trust I will be okay, and things will fall into their rightful order.'

Affirmation 267

Truth must be what we try to live by. If we lie, we lose the ability of our words advocating for us in place of our actions. Telling the truth is the insurance we pay for the accusations of tomorrow.

'I stand for truth. I stand by my word. My word is my bond. I am honest. I have integrity. My word can be relied on.'

Affirmation 268

What is that one thing that makes you feel vulnerable and exposed? That thing you pray nobody ever finds out? Why does that thing have so much power over you? Confront it and challenge it. Take back your power.

'I will not let anything I have experienced or done tarnish where I am today. I am not the only person with a story. I will build my confidence up to get to a place where I am comfortable with all elements of my past.'

Affirmation 269

Trust your instincts when you feel they're trying to tell you something. Don't explain away the evidence of what your spirit is communicating to you. Just because it's uncomfortable doesn't make it invalid. Believe what you feel.

'I trust myself enough to accept what my soul is telling me. I do not need to see physical evidence or receive the validation of others to validate myself. I have the ability to hear clearly what words are not telling me.'

Affirmation 270

Change is a wonderful thing, but change must be managed. If we don't manage the change that we want to see, it just becomes reckless action, disjointed and incoherent, and it will not bring us the results we desire.

'I am methodical and deliberate in how I manage and apply change. I am coherent. I am orderly. I am structured. I will manage the process of the change I want to see and the change I am ready for.'

Affirmation 271

Independence is power. The moment you aren't reliant on another emotionally, financially or physically, your life is your own. The only exception is if those you rely on truly see themselves as servants acting in love and not masters of your destiny.

'I am not afraid to stand alone. I see everyone who is helping me as a helper and not a saviour. I put my trust in something more powerful than myself so I will not be afraid or indebted in ways that are unhealthy or ways that stop me from believing I can stand on my own two feet.'

Affirmation 272

Don't judge a journey you haven't been on. It's easy to have an opinion on a pain you have not felt or an experience you have not had. What bridges the pain of another to what you have never gone through is compassion. Feel it and embrace it; only then can you be there for others.

'I am a safe space for those who confide in me. I do not dismiss what I cannot feel, but I will extend a hand of love and friendship to those who choose me to share in their healing journey. I give peace and love to those in need.'

Affirmation 273

Take a moment to take in the things you see around you. Look at what you have against what you want and need. You may not have all you want, but you have enough for today. Let gratitude and thanksgiving fill you whilst you are in a state of expectation of what your heart desires.

'I don't take for granted the gift of sight. I am grateful for what I have around me. I may not have it all, but I have all I need, and I am thankful. I open myself to receive more of what my heart wants.'

Affirmation 274

Making amends is a great show of strength, yet it shows great humility, too. It takes a lot to admit where we have messed up and arrive at a place where we take the responsibility to put things right. It shows growth. Well done for allowing yourself to grow.

'I will not allow pride to ruin my relationships. I will make the effort to put myself in the other person's shoes to show I know how my actions may have hurt them. I am a working on being a better person. I will make mistakes, but I will put them right, too. I value people, so I will treat them well.'

Affirmation 275

What is stopping you from putting your plans into action? What is stopping you from realising your full potential? Is it fear, finances, lack of know-how? None of these things should stop you. Though they might delay you, they cannot deny you. Be deliberate and make it happen.

'I will not give up. If I'm knocked down seven times, seven times, I will rise. My journey will not be without setbacks and knockbacks. I am ready for the journey. I will make it, come what may.'

Affirmation 276

What emotions are you not comfortable expressing? Why? Each emotion we feel, we feel for a reason. Try and take the time to analyse why you feel what you feel and when you feel it. To be emotionally independent means you are in control of your feelings, and that means you are in control of how you express them and not the other way around.

'I will be mature in how I display my feelings. I will not deny what shows up for me emotionally. Everything I experience is to make me more balanced. I will do the work to be emotionally balanced, so all my relationships will benefit from the new me.'

Affirmation 277

*E*ver heard the term 'Better late than never'? When you think about it, is anything ever really late? Or is it that we think we're ready for things before their time? Maybe the things we wish for are right on time, and it's us who are late in realising that.

'I trust that what is for me, what is due to me, will come right on time. I will not waste time fretting and willing things to manifest before their time. I will trust that what is for me will know when I am ready. I will continue to prepare myself for the things I hope for, the things I have not yet seen but believe I will receive.'

Affirmation 278

Sharing what we have, be it in knowledge, time or money, can give us a real sense of meaning to our lives. We can always enjoy what we have alone, but seeing the appreciation on the faces of those who benefit from our kindness and generosity isn't to be underestimated. Somebody somewhere is waiting for something only you can give.

'I will share with others what I have been blessed with. I will be a channel of manifestation for those who need me. I am happy to be of service to others.'

Affirmation 279

Making up can be hard. Maybe we are the aggrieved party, or maybe we are the ones who have caused the pain. Think of how much you care for yourself and the one who is hurt, and don't let pride get in the way just because it's hard to reconcile and move forward. Life is always one step at a time.

'I may need time to process how I feel, but I will take the time to understand my emotions. I will not allow things to fester. I will be adult. I will be calm. I will articulate my feelings well because it is important I am heard. It is important I hear. It is important we heal.'

Affirmation 280

Do you feel you have been short-changed in life? Do you feel there's a lot more out there than you are experiencing? Maybe you're right! The question is, what do you intend to do about it? Time to act and stop looking at the coins in your hands. Go get what is yours.

'I will not complain and remain stagnant. I will go for what I know I can achieve. I will give life my best shot and live life without regret.'

Affirmation 281

Who looks up to you? You're somebody's idol. You're somebody's idea of what good looks like. Don't take your silent audience for granted, the ones who look up to you that you aren't aware of. You are still winning after all you've been through, and it's spurring them on. You are an example of what is possible. Keep going, and well done.

'I know my pain has not been in vain. I have not gone through all my life's experiences for nothing. I am still here to tell the tale. I am still standing. I will carry others along with me. I am, indeed, an example of what is possible. Victory is possible.'

Affirmation 282

Putting yourself first is often deemed as selfish, but sometimes, you need to do that for the sake of your wellbeing. Walking away isn't just a lesson for the other person; it's a lesson for you, too.

'I do not apologise for choosing me over the disrespect, the pain and the disappointment. I give myself permission to make me a priority over all that is negative and does not serve me. I am worth all that I wish for.'

Affirmation 283

Whatever negativity you may be feeling in this moment, let it wash over you. No matter its source or origin, close your eyes and let it pass. Don't argue with it; don't reason with it; let it pass. Your voice needs to be the loudest in this moment, countering the negative feelings and thoughts at this present time.

'I am not my negative thoughts. I am not what my experiences expect me to be. I am all things good. I am all things positive. I am all things beautiful.'

Affirmation 284

Never get tired of doing good. It can get difficult when you don't get any thanks but don't do it because of the thanks. Do good because of you.

'I do good because it is in my calling to do so. I am not selective in who I choose to bless. I am a giver of all things good. I do what I do because it makes me happy and warms my heart to do so.'

Affirmation 285

We all make mistakes. Don't go through life trying to avoid them. You lose so many opportunities for growth by trying to avoid being human. Relax. Don't worry about what might go wrong. Embrace all that will go right after those mistakes and those you can help from what you've learnt.

'I am not trying to be perfect; I am learning to be human. I will make mistakes, but they will not define me. I will learn from what I get wrong and what I do or say wrong. I will put right my wrongs and embrace my growth along the way.'

Affirmation 286

There are going to be days when you just don't want to get out of bed. The tasks of the day, last night's disagreement with a loved one, all the bills due without enough money to cover them…yeah, I get it. I understand. Then, you remember people are relying on you. Your partner, your spouse, your kids, your parents, the job, your clients…and then there's you. You're relying on you. You've got to dig deep. You can't let you down.

'I've had better days, and today is a better day because I say so. I believe it will be because I say so. It's not a perfect day, but it's a good day because I say so. So, today, I'm going to take a deep breath and carry on, and I'll be okay because I say so.'

Affirmation 287

If you had it, you've still got it. Don't ever believe that you can lose your gifts and talents. All that is needed is for you to be in the right environment at the right time and with the right people to bring out what is in you. Greatness can never be lost; it can only be hidden but never buried.

'I am great. I am endowed with gifts and talents hidden in me, yet to be discovered and used. I believe the gifts and talents within me will create the right opportunities for me to shine. I am ready.'

Affirmation 288

It is always good to do a friendship roll call. Who is present, and who is absent? People change, and friends are people, so expect it. There are those who start off as loyal but turn out to be your greatest, secret enemy. Don't worry—it's all part of life's lessons to keep us on our toes and to let us know what not to be to others.

'Friends come and friends go. I will remember the good times and move on. I will not be bitter. I will move forward, taking note of all the lessons I have learnt.'

Affirmation 289

As life changes, so should we. Be adaptable. Learn to function and operate when the tide changes. Don't be lost when you have limited funds, or you are not able to show up as you would normally. The more adaptable you are to changing situations, the less change will affect you negatively.

'I am content in all stages and states of my life. Whether I have money or not, whether I am alone or not, whether I have to walk instead of drive. No matter my situation or circumstance, I am grateful.'

Affirmation 290

If you happen to be grieving anyone or something deeply, it's just testament to the depths of how deeply you can love. As painful as that may be, know that it is, indeed, better to have loved and lost than never to have loved at all.

'My heart may be full of pain, but it is also full of love. I will learn how to experience joy amidst the pain and allow time to heal me and give me memories that I can cherish without sadness or regret.'

Affirmation 291

Don't knock getting older. Therein lies the confidence you so lacked in your younger days, and if you didn't, it will come, and it will grow. Share your journey with others and help them navigate their lives with fewer setbacks or delays because you have been there, done that. Yes, getting older is all that it's cracked up to be. It's awesome.

'I will enjoy all the days I have been blessed with. I am not afraid of my future. I live a full and happy life that can and will only get better. I am in charge of my joy and happiness.'

Affirmation 292

Be careful of the burdens you carry. Some will leave you with aches and pains, others, a broken back, and a few can even leave you crippled. Being a help to those in need is commendable and admirable, but if it leaves you flattened and deflated, that burden isn't for you. Take care of your back.

'I will give what I can, but I will not forget about myself. I am empathetic, and I am kind and loyal, but I will not let these traits take precedence over my wellbeing. I am important. I will not be a burden to myself.'

Affirmation 293

Most children are afraid of the dark because they don't know what's in the darkness. We grow, and we see darkness in so many things around us. We don't need to fear. We have access to that light switch. Flick it on and see that it was just the shadows, giving the illusion that there were monsters in the dark.

'Fear is far from me. I am bold, and I am brave. I will not imagine there is anything that can overcome me. I will deal with my fears head-on. I am in control. I am fearless'

Affirmation 294

Step your game up! Once you've achieved what you set out to achieve, set yourself a new challenge and stretch yourself a little more. The more you stretch yourself, the less likely you will ever be bored with life. You will experience all it has to offer, so keep moving and keep achieving even greater goals.

'I am a go-getter! I will live life to the fullest and will be unapologetic in doing so.

I will not rest and be complacent. I will challenge myself mentally, and I will keep my mind alive and vibrant.'

Affirmation 295

The idle mind is the devil's workshop. A mind that is dormant, unchallenged and unstimulated is open season for unhealthy, unproductive and damaging thoughts to take residence. Keep your mind active, and your body will follow suit. Do that and make your soul smile.

'I will not allow my mind to be unstimulated. I will fill my mind with thoughts of how I can better myself, thoughts of how I can add value to others and healthy thoughts that help my wellbeing. Thoughts that are unkind to myself and others, I will not feed or entertain. My mind is active. My mind is a workshop for all that is good and pure.'

Affirmation 296

Que sera sera, whatever will be will be. Will it? Throwing caution to the wind isn't always the best. You don't know which direction the wind will blow. Take some control by being deliberate in what you want to do and how you want to do it.

'I am clear and deliberate in what I want to manifest. If I think it, I can will it into being. I am not going to allow the elements to determine where I fall. I will always land firmly on my feet in pleasant places.'

Affirmation 297

*E*ach talent we have is to bless someone as well as ourselves. The more we have, the greater the people we have been called to enrich their lives. Nothing that you possess is little or small. For the right audience, you are all they need. For the right audience, you are enough.

'What I carry inside me isn't small. What I have to offer isn't insignificant. I am perfect for the people I have been called to. I will never judge who I am by the standards of those who do not know me. I understand you cannot appreciate what you don't know. I know. I appreciate me.'

Affirmation 298

They say people change when they come into money; not true. Can you imagine trying to throw your weight around without money in your pocket? No, people don't really change; they just need the right climate to exhibit what was always there. Self-reflection is always a must. Don't let circumstances change you for the worse; you change circumstances for the better.

'I am working towards fitting into what my future holds for me. I am in training for the things I hope for. I will not change for the worse. The manifestation of the things I desire will make me and others better. I am ready.'

Affirmation 299

Brace yourself. Just before the finishing line is where you will meet your toughest challenge and the most reasons to give up. Don't give up. Look at how far you've come. Keep your eyes to the sky. Don't look down. There is a mighty cheer waiting for you at the finish line. That cheer will come from you.

'I will keep on pushing. I will not give up. I will not crumble. I have come too far to turn back now. I will imagine the feeling I will experience from a deep sense of achievement. I will hold onto that feeling. I will not let it go.'

Affirmation 300

Goodbyes are painful, but at times, they are necessary. Closing the door on the old and making way for the new. Releasing people and things to go on their own path as you go onto yours. Cry a little and smile; the change is for your good.

'I will work through the pain and disappointments that have come my way. I will be hopeful for my future, knowing it's time to look forward with anticipation that better things are on the way for me.'

Affirmation 301

Keep your eyes open, your ears peeled and your lips sealed. Not everything requires a response. All you need do is pay attention and let things unfold. At times, holding your cards close to your chest is the best way to deal with certain situations life throws at you.

'I am not reactive to adverse situations. I possess enough self-control to observe and take in what I see because I am in control. I respond intentionally and intelligently to what is presented to me.'

Affirmation 302

It is difficult to walk in synch with people if we are not in agreement with them. Being on the same page with those we want to grow with is crucial. Take time to communicate the things that are important to you and which direction you want to go in. Find those who buy into your vision and walk in time with them, after finding common ground.

'I communicate my needs clearly. I know where I am going, and I know who I want to go with. I am open and reasonable to hear the concerns of those I want on my team.'

Affirmation 303

We all make mistakes. Nobody is beyond getting things wrong, but don't condemn yourself. No matter what has gone wrong or how much you feel you've messed up, you don't have to write yourself off. Your story is still unfolding.

'The chapters in my life are still unfolding. I believe my story will end well. I will not put my book down. I will keep on reading, each page more exciting and full of promise than the last.'

Affirmation 304

Allow people to grow. Let them have their moment of messing up and making mistakes. Sometimes, you have to let them go and find themselves so they can be themselves.

'As I grow, I will let others grow. I will not hold onto anyone so tightly that I will not allow them to be who they need to be. I will not put my needs above theirs. I will be a source of support for those finding their way.'

Affirmation 305

There are many seasons of life, and some may be times that you feel sadness. You can't expect happy days all the time because that is not real life. It really is okay to feel that way; just don't stay in a place that becomes a never ending day of sadness. Look after yourself, and you will find your happy.

'I am on many journeys, and I am okay with the seasons of life I am going through. I may not feel happy today, but I will ride the wave and settle into a place of happiness.'

Affirmation 306

Discover the purpose of your existence. Only then will you find fulfilment and the true meaning of life. Too many of us don't know why we're here, and we end up chasing people, things and dreams that were never meant for us. If there is a reason for you being here, there is a unique purpose for you to fulfil. Find it, and live it.

'I will take time to find my true calling. I will not settle, and I will not be frustrated. I will embrace all that I am. I will take note and welcome every experience and encounter that comes my way because I know it is helping me on my way to discovery.'

Affirmation 307

*E*very day is a special occasion. The moment you wake up is a day of celebration. Don't wait to pop the Champagne, or wear that special outfit or visit that swanky restaurant. Just enjoy life. Don't put off your day of celebration; today is a good day to enjoy life.

'I will not put off any opportunities to revel in the moment. I will not put off treating myself to the things I enjoy. I am so worth it.'

Affirmation 308

They say you can't help who you fall in love with, but we all possess the power and strength to choose friends and loved ones wisely. We only need to find that thing in us that draws us to pain and destruction, and once we deal with it, the right love will be drawn to us.

'I will be intentional about the people I choose to have in my circle. I will not give my power to manage my emotions to anyone who will not do as good a job as me. I am my own keeper. I will keep myself for the right people at the right time.'

Affirmation 309

Change tactics if what you're doing isn't working. It's okay to be wrong. Don't let pride make you carry on doing what isn't bringing you the results you want. Don't let the fear of others saying 'I told you so' deter you from calling time on what you're doing. Go away, rethink, regroup and come back better than before. You have it in you.

'My end goal is to succeed. I will seek advice from the right people to help me on that road to success. I am not designed for delay. I will not prolong my journey in getting where I need to go. I will not be a hinderance to myself.'

Affirmation 310

Be realistic about the harvest you're expecting. What seeds have you sown? What have you planted, and what conditions have you created for your seeds to bear fruit? Each seed has its time to germinate. Don't watch to see how, or when the seed sprouts. The elements will take care of it.

'I am conscious of every seed I sow. I have invested well. I will allow the right time to bring forth the fruit from the seeds I have planted. No seed of mine will fall on bad ground. I will be expectant.'

Affirmation 311

Keep in touch with reality. It's so easy to forget when we are not living the life of others. Feed the poor, speak to the homeless and see the world through their eyes. It will always keep you grounded and grateful.

'I don't take for granted the things I have. I am grateful that my story, though tough, is bearable. I will extend my hand of hope to others because I know, but for the grace of God, there go I.'

Affirmation 312

Be open to new ideas and new ways of thinking. The world is ever-changing and challenging us in so many ways. As the world evolves, so must our thinking; not necessarily to agree, but to expose us to challenge our values and see if we are holding the right ones.

'I am open to change. I am not afraid of my value system being challenged. I know I can stand by my convictions because I am true to myself in every situation.'

Affirmation 313

Don't be in a hurry all the time. Don't rush life. Soak it all in and appreciate those moments that are gone too soon. Slow down and enjoy the moment that you are in.

'Right now, I am soaking up the air I breathe, the things I see with my eyes and in my mind's eye. I appreciate life. I will continue to live it on purpose.'

Affirmation 314

Trust yourself but not so much that you don't give yourself space to make mistakes. Nobody is perfect all of the time; it's a learning curve. Practice makes perfect, so keep trusting yourself, but learn from your mistakes, and you will master the art of trusting your instincts in no time.

'I am learning, and I am doing well. I can see where I have gone wrong. I will not make the same mistakes twice. I will listen to my inner voice.'

Affirmation 315

Believe beyond what you can see because no matter how good our sight is, we cannot rely on it. What we dream and what we believe really resides in our hearts.

'I will believe with my heart and not with my eyes. I may see but not comprehend that there is good that is hidden amongst the bad. I may see the facts with my eyes, but I see the truth with my heart.'

Affirmation 316

Never be afraid to walk away from toxic people, no matter how much you feel you can't survive without them. It's all an illusion. If you get the support you need and learn to stand on your own two feet, learn that you have all it takes because you were born complete, you will be able to let them go, no matter who they are.

'I am okay on my own. I can cope on my own. I can manage on my own. I can be happy on my own. I will not give my power to anyone to validate me. I validate me on my own.'

Affirmation 317

Are you always late? Are you always the last to show up? How about you imagine you have a really important date with you? So much is riding on you being present. It may take a bit of practice but learn to be at the right place at the right time. You never know what you might miss by being late.

'I will plan my time well. I will honour the invitations and places I need to be on time for, as a sign of respect for myself and others.'

Affirmation 318

Emotional intelligence is so important. Being able to read and validate the emotions of others, as well as ourselves, and labelling them correctly really helps our relationships to thrive. Train yourself to be in tune with emotions; it will help you read the rooms you enter.

'I am emotionally alert to my own feelings and others. I am aware of the emotions in and around me. I pay attention to keep safe and to know when to retreat. I am emotionally intelligent. I am emotionally aware. I am a safe haven for myself and other people.'

Affirmation 319

Allow the metamorphosis to do its job. You don't need to know in fine detail what's taking place; just know that it is beautiful and trust the process.

'I welcome every stage of my existence. I may not understand what's going on at every stage, but I choose to believe that each change will bring out the best in me. Each change will empower me for the next stage of my life.'

Affirmation 320

Commitment requires commitment. There are no shortcuts to getting done what we need to get done. Commitment requires commitment.

'I am ready to press in. I am ready to take the plunge; no turning back or modifying what I want because of procrastination or lack of focus. I am committed to the dream. I am committed to my cause.'

Affirmation 321

Fashion, image, what's hot and what's not is ever-changing. Stick to your own style, and don't try to look like anyone else. Don't try to be anyone else. All these things change, but who you are must remain constant. Stay true to you. That will always be in vogue.

'I am comfortable in my own skin. I don't conform to trends to define who I am. I am uniquely and stylishly me. I am never out of fashion. I am always current.'

Affirmation 322

Align with what you want to see manifest in your life. Be around the things you want to see. Invest in those who are showing up and living what you are waiting to experience. They're all seeds. They will yield a harvest for you.

'I will seek out those who are where I am aspiring to be. I will cheer them on, and I will learn from them. I will appreciate and celebrate their success, knowing, in the fullness of time, I will be celebrated too.'

Affirmation 323

*E*ncourage someone and spur them on. You have no idea how your words can be what someone needs to hear. Your words that will stop them from giving up and keep going just because of you.

'I know my words are powerful. I know I hold great authority when I speak my words over others. I choose to use my words wisely, with compassion and to build and not destroy.'

Affirmation 324

Break away from people and things that hinder your progress. We are not all on the same journey or finishing at the same time. Join yourself to those who are ready to keep up or lead the way, not mark time and hold you back.

'I am on a mission. I will accomplish my mission with the right people to help my focus, commitments and dreams. I will not be sentimental and hold onto those I need to let go.'

Affirmation 325

Don't hide who you really are. If you're proud of you, shine for the world to see. You were created to be a light to shine. Don't shrink or hide the true you. You are the missing component in someone's story.

'I will be bold and stand out. I am not going to diminish who I am by hiding who I am. What I have inside me is what the world needs. I am meant to stand out.'

Affirmation 326

If you're on a journey, and you've made it halfway to your destination, keep going. The strength you need has already been proven to exist inside of you. You have undisputed evidence of what you're made of; it's definitely the stuff of winners.

'I have what it takes to complete my course. I know if I really focus, I can get to where I need to go. If I can complete the first half, I have it in me to complete the rest. Throwing in the towel is not an option. Flying the flag of victory is.'

Affirmation 327

Don't wait for a new year to embark on a new beginning. A new day presents the same opportunities. A change in your mindset is all you need to put the wheels in motion, not a date in a calendar.

'If I want something new, I will go for it. I will focus and prepare myself to alter the areas of my life where I want to see newness. I will not wait.'

Affirmation 328

Life positions each and every one of us where it wills. Depending on where we are in life, we may have to do certain jobs or live in certain places because that's our level at the time. These things should not define us, and they most certainly should not be the yardstick used to determine whether we should be treated well or not. No matter where we are in life, we should never feel beneath or below anyone.

'I treat everyone I come across with dignity and respect. From waiters to CEOs, I do not make any distinction between people. We all are of value, and everybody is a somebody. I choose to treat people well because I expect that in return.'

Affirmation 329

The outside world can appear too noisy, and you can't hear yourself think. It's OKAY to withdraw, take time out to clear your mind, and look at things with a fresh pair of eyes. Remember to say that you need time out so those around you can respect your space and allow you to be.

'I will retreat to a place where I can reset and recharge. I will find a place that gives me clarity of thought. I don't have to keep going with clouded thoughts and jumbled emotions. I will be back, recentred, reset and refocused.'

Affirmation 330

*E*xperience is said to be the best teacher, but experience can also promote fear and retard your progress. One bad experience doesn't guarantee another. Learn what you have to, but don't let fear be instilled in you as part of that experience.

'I will extract the lessons that I need to learn from each experience, leaving out the fear that tries to attach itself to what I have gone through. My experiences make me stronger, not weaker, and I will thrive with what life has thrown at me.'

Affirmation 331

Get your mind out of the way! Stop overthinking and getting in the way of life. We were never meant to know everything. We are, however, meant to take chances, take a leap of faith and hope for the best.

'I will ride on the waves of life. I will take life where it leads me and stop trying to control what is out of my reach. I will not try to tell the future; I will only prepare for it in whichever way I can. I will not allow the unknown to rob me of my joy.'

Affirmation 332

Send the elevator back down and help someone who is trying to get to where you are. It doesn't have to be lonely at the top if there are enough of you there.

'I will create spaces for those who will come after me. I am not afraid of who may overtake me. My objective is to leave wherever I find myself in a better state than I found it. My hope is to leave people greater than I am.'

Affirmation 333

Repetition is good. Sometimes we need to learn something more than once. We increase faith in ourselves by hearing what we need over and over. So don't say, 'Oh, I've heard it all before!' Sometimes, you need to hear how great you are more than once to really believe it.

'I will keep reminding myself that I am fabulous. I will unashamedly describe myself with all the great adjectives I can find to seep into my body, mind and soul until I believe it, even when the outside world says otherwise.'

Affirmation 334

What do you draw on for strength? Everyone has a source. How solid is that strength, and can it take your weight? Don't reach out to anyone who doesn't have the muscle power to hold you in the moments you need to be held.

'I will be discerning and careful with whom I reach out to for help. I will watch who I allow to carry me in my time of need. I will not place an unfair expectation on anybody who doesn't have the capacity to bear my weight when I need them.'

Affirmation 335

Have you started your daily walks? How does it feel to have that thinking and focus time all to yourself? Taking a daily walk is good for your health, too, especially if you are pressed for time and don't get to exercise much. You deserve to carve out time that is just for you to be with your thoughts.

'It is important for me to have the time and space to think, strategise and reflect. I will make time for me and get physical exercise into my daily routine to help keep my mind and body the best they can be.'

Affirmation 336

*L*earn to adapt, no matter your circumstances. Know how to manage yourself in whatever state you find yourself. You will find that less can control you and dictate your mood when you are not swayed or influenced by things out of your control.

'I am resilient and strong. I stand firm and grounded in peace of mind. In whatever state I find myself, I know I will be okay. I am okay.'

Affirmation 337

The falling rain is a beautiful thing to the farmer needing to water their crops, but not so for the person who has just stepped out of the hairdresser's without an umbrella, having spent a fortune. The rain didn't change; the people did. How we respond to what life throws at us just depends on where we are. Never stop loving life or the rain.

'I will appreciate the rain. I will appreciate where I am when it falls. I will respond with gratitude, whatever the case. I am a vessel of thankfulness in every situation.'

Affirmation 338

Shine the light on others; it doesn't dim your shine in the least. Let others have their moment. They will thank you for it, and it will show how secure you are in who you are.

'I will gladly boast about the greatness of others. In celebrating their greatness, we become great together. Together, we can do amazing things if we are in one accord. I will always be the first to uplift those who are doing their best.'

Affirmation 339

Being in a relationship, if it's healthy, is a wonderful thing. Being one half of a union that you have chosen to be in is great, but we must never lose a sense of who we are. It's our responsibility to grow and be better as individuals. We create more beautiful relationships when we better ourselves.

'My growth is my responsibility. My evolution is not my partner's or anyone else's responsibility. I will not remain emotionally or mentally stagnant. I will grow into the fullness of my true self.'

Affirmation 340

*P*rotecting your mental health requires deliberate action. What are you doing to keep it healthy? Try and stay away from people who create stress and anxiety in you. Keep away from environments that make you feel unsafe and vulnerable. You are the caretaker of you, so please take care.

'I am under no obligation to stay anywhere that my mental health is going to suffer. I will be deliberate in avoiding places or people who are not good for me.'

Affirmation 341

Healing is a process, so stop rushing it. You can't will a wound to heal. Every second of every minute, hour and day, that wound is healing behind the scenes, and it begins to show this by not bleeding anymore. Give yourself time. Different wounds take different times to heal. Be patient.

'I will allow the process to take whatever path it chooses. The end result is assured. I will focus on the prize. I will not be distracted by the pain. I will wait patiently until I am whole.'

Affirmation 342

New relationships are exciting, but instead of putting your best foot forward, be your authentic self. Let people know you are what it says on the tin.

'I am happy and confident in the person I present myself to be. What you see is what you get. Truth, honesty and a pure and clean spirit. I only have the one version of myself, and it is good.'

Affirmation 343

Only the one standing behind you can tell you the line you are drawing is crooked. Perspective is sometimes better gained when you take a step back. It's good to hear the views of those who are honest and have our best interests at heart. They can often see what's too close to us to see. Listen.

'I will not rely solely on my wisdom when I have a problem to solve, need advice or when I am embarking on the journey of the unknown. I will seek counsel and advice from those who have my best interests at heart and will never shy away from telling me the truth because I can handle the truth.'

Affirmation 344

There's a Ghanaian adage that says, 'When the calf is bigger than the thigh, it's because the leg is diseased.' Give credit to those who have gone before you because there's much to learn from them. Humility is a great ingredient when gaining wisdom and knowledge from the more experienced and seasoned amongst us.

'I will honour and respect those who have earned their stripes. I am not too proud to sit and receive the wisdom of those who have gone through more to teach me more.'

Affirmation 345

Friends come and go, and sometimes, it's hard to let go. You can't force someone to be your friend, but you can always ensure you're the best friend a person could ask for. Be a friend to those who need one of your two shoulders to lean or cry on; they're broad enough. When they lean on you, you can lean on them. In that moment, it's about what you can give more than what you can receive.

'I want today to be about giving someone who needs a little light to have me shine mine on them. I know how it feels to need someone but can find no one. Even if it means making eye contact with a stranger on the bus or passing a stranger in the office hallway or the person in the shop, I'll be that friend today and just nod my head and smile.'

Affirmation 346

Who is your wingman? Who is your co-pilot? Check that they are qualified for the position. Were they fast-tracked into the job, or did they earn it? Did you check their credentials? Any training required? The position of a best friend can make or break you. Make sure they pass the test before being left in post.

'I only attract good-spirited souls to be around me. I will be unbiased in my assessment of those in my circle, never afraid to let go of those who have run their course. I will always leave room for new hearts to come into my life.'

Affirmation 347

Don't let the giants in your promised land frighten you. They're there for two reasons: 1. To ask you how much you want to enter it, and 2. To never be bullied into giving up what is yours. So, what is it going to be?

'I will not be intimidated by challenges. I will not be fearful of the fight I need to put up to enter into what is mine. Yes, I really want it. Yes, I will fight for it. Yes, I will win.'

Affirmation 348

Don't forget where you came from. The experiences you've overcome are waiting to be heard by those needing to overcome the same struggles. Don't be silent; your voice is the key to unlocking someone's prison.

'I will not hide my past. There is nothing I have gone through that was not for a reason. There is somebody who made what I have been through worth it. I am thankful my pain is not in vain.'

Affirmation 349

Sometimes, the truth is hard to swallow, but to move forward, we need to face the truth. We can't live a lie and still live a full life. You will know the truth, and the truth shall make you free.

'I will not be afraid of the truth. I will embrace it. I will not be afraid or run from it. If the truth grants me my freedom, I will not shy away from the things I need to know. I would rather live in truth than remain in bondage from lies.'

Affirmation 350

What's your motive for the things you do for others? Is it for thanks? Is it for praise? Or do you just enjoy being good to others? Relish that feeling if that is your motivation. Giving of yourself to help people is never in vain if you give of yourself to the right people.

'My motives are always honourable when I offer to help someone. I seek nothing in return, not gratitude nor indebtedness. My desire is that they pay it forward to help create love and support for one another.'

Affirmation 351

Build on a solid foundation, and when the tests and trials of life come, the winds and the rains will not destroy what you've built. The more solid the building, the deeper you'll have to dig for the foundation. So, take time to dig deep. A good investment that will bring you great gains.

'Spending time to create a solid foundation is my insurance to enjoy the things I build. I will not cut corners. I will invest what I need to appreciate the fruits of my labour because I will never labour in vain.'

Affirmation 352

Not all help is helpful. An extended hand that appears to pull you up but is really pressing you down is to be avoided at all costs. Never let desperation cloud your judgement or ability to discern those who are against you. True and honest help is out there. Wait for it; it's coming.

'I have the power to discern the intentions of those around me. I will not allow my needs to lead me to a place where I will be taken advantage of. I will not end up in a place where I am not looked on with love, compassion and respect. I will draw only true helpers to me.'

Affirmation 353

Deal with your demons when nobody else is watching. Don't suppress the things you struggle with instead of dealing with them head-on. If it's anger issues, insecurity, poor money management—whatever it is, deal with it privately. Don't fall in front of an audience and be forced to change. Shame is never a good motivation for change.

'I will face my demons head-on. I will not make excuses. I will not justify them. I will not lie to myself. I have an area of growth I need to deal with, so I do so in all humility. I will go through the process. As painful and as uncomfortable as it might be, I am ready.'

Affirmation 354

Take a breather from all the balls you're juggling. You can defy gravity. Leave them suspended in the air for a moment; they'll wait for you to come back and pick up from where you left off.

'I don't ever need to be overwhelmed by the many things that demand my time and attention. The world won't stop turning because I stop doing. I am allowed to step aside for a moment to catch my breath. I will be deliberate in making time for me.'

Affirmation 355

It's hard to let go, but we need to understand that people have the right to change the rules of the game. Whether it's us or a loved one, give them and yourself that space and chance to be what you all need to be, even without each other.

'Letting go may be hard, but I have the strength of mind and soul to untie my soul from those who have reached the end of their journey with me. I wish them well. I wish myself well. I will not be bitter; I will be better. I am okay. It's all working for my good.'

Affirmation 356

Don't turn your nose up at starting small. It takes care of the sense of overwhelm and the feeling you're not doing enough regarding that big dream. Celebrate the daily wins, weekly wins, monthly wins, and in no time, you'll see how much you've achieved a year on. Start small; it's really big of you to do so.

'Slow and steady wins the race. I am not in competition with anyone. I have my own lane that I am thriving in. I will pat myself on the back and encourage myself. A win is a win, and I continue to win in all areas of my life.'

Affirmation 357

Be with someone who you want, not who you need. A need speaks of dependency. Nobody should be a drug to you. Be whole and be happy all by yourself. That's the best and only version that is ready for love, life and commitment.

'I am enough all by myself. Anyone I choose to be a part of my life will come to enhance it, not define it. I am truly, honestly, sincerely enough all by myself.'

Affirmation 358

Sometimes, we are so eager to have something or someone that we rarely stop and take a minute to ask ourselves if we are ready for what we want. The greater the expectation, the greater the preparation. Don't be too eager to get what you aren't ready for. Don't pray for what you cannot sustain.

'I will not be in a hurry to get what I am not ready for. I will not despise the many ways I am being tried and tested to qualify for the things my heart desires, whether it is love, a change, a move. I will sustain and maintain all good things coming my way. The days of loss and disappointment are over.'

Affirmation 359

The outward appearances we see of people aren't always an indication of who they are inside. The heart is well hidden under appearances and a pile of clothes. The clothes don't make the man; the heart does. Look for that and save yourself a lot of disappointment.

'I will look beyond the surface to really get to know the people around me. I will not be swayed by the outward appearances of what I see. I will look much deeper. I will be conscious of my own heart and what's really there.'

Affirmation 360

Don't criticise in others what you haven't fixed in yourself. Yes, pick out the log from your own eye before picking out the speck in another's. We are all fighting battles unique to the journey we are on. Be kind and show compassion. We are all at war, fighting for the same side…we are just in different uniforms.

'I work on myself to be better. I extend that same grace to others, not to compare or compete, but to understand that change for us all is hard. I will keep trying and will help others to win their battles, too.'

Affirmation 361

Everything in life comes at a cost, it just depends on what you are willing to pay. We chase all sorts of things in the quest to fulfil our version of what a good life looks like. Money, fame, a quiet life, family; the list is endless. What are you willing to pay for the life you want to live?

'I am dedicated and committed to the things I want in my life. I am prepared to put the work in and get the results I deserve. Giving up is not an option. Giving in is not my desire. I have the spirit of tenacity. I will work hard, I will work smart, and I will accomplish all I set out to achieve.'

Affirmation 362

Shut off and shut down days are necessary. Necessary for you to gather your thoughts, recharge your batteries and focus on you. Don't feel guilty. Don't let your mind battle you to bring thoughts that will not allow you to relax. To be at your best, shut down, shut off and shut out days are a must.

'I give myself permission to log out of the world for a minute. I am important. My health is important. My mind is important. My whole being is important. I will take the time I need to recharge and refocus to be great again.'

Affirmation 363

When we don't know the purpose or the value of a thing, it is subject to misuse or abuse. What is it that is being misused or abused in your life? What are you misusing and abusing? Your time, your looks, your gifts, your talents? Everything you possess has a divine purpose. Find it, put it to good use, and let it work for you.

'Whatever I possess, I will take care of and make sure I use it to its full potential. I will take my time to consciously look at all that I have and make sure I am accountable. I will not misuse anything I have been blessed with.'

Affirmation 364

Free your mind and do some decluttering. Where should the bad memories be placed? How can you file the happy thoughts that you need to go to in times of sadness? Where can you find the things you need in your mind to keep it alert, healthy and free from stress and anxiety? It's time for a clear-out. Let's get to work.

'I free my mind from thoughts that cloud my judgement, my ability to be present, and my ability to be in control. I will dictate what takes residence in my thoughts. I will have a mind clear of what doesn't promote my emotional, mental or spiritual wellbeing.'

Affirmation 365

The end doesn't necessarily spell the end. It just means an end to an event, a path or an era. New things are born after things end. Embrace the era of new beginnings and new adventures. Look ahead. The light is there. It will lead you, and it will guide you. *365 Ways to Tell You You're Special,* because quite simply you are. There is no one like you. Don't ever feel you are not wanted, or you are dispensable because you are not; you just need to shine in the right places. A Rolls Royce is an excellent car, but it's of little use in a cycling race. Find your place in life and enjoy the ride. It must feel pretty special that you're the ONLY person who has ever walked on the face of the Earth that can do what you were created to do, in the way that you will do it.

Go on and enjoy the awesome life that's waiting for you…

'I am special in 365 ways. Every single day, I will recognise how special I am. I will not forget. I believe the words I have spoken over my existence, over my world and over my desires. There really is no one like me. I am created for peace, joy, greatness, and to fulfil my destiny. I am truly special every single day of the year.'

Acknowledgments

Thank you to my daughter Isobel, who validated these words by asking to hear them every morning. Meant so much to me.

Thank you for the unwavering love, support and prayers of New Glory Ministry, especially Apostle Isaac Olujide who has pushed me beyond limits to know I have no limit.

Bishop Folashade Kolawole, what can I say? Your words put my pen back in my hand to write again. My heart will always be grateful.

To Daniella Blechner my publisher… you make writing from the heart a breeze. Thank you for creating the space for me to speak into the lives and hearts of people.

About the Author

Dilys is a qualified and accredited transformational life coach, women and children's advocate, a public and TEDx speaker, events host and MC, as well as a minister at New Glory Ministry in London.

She is the bestselling author of the book, 'Not This Widow', a story of resilience and defiance in the face of profound grief. She is also the author of 'Predator or Prince - How To Find The Man Of Your Dreams, Not Your Nightmares', a book that teaches women and girls how to spot red flags in abusive relationships.

Dilys is also the host of her own show, 'Speak With Dilys', aired via Facebook and TV. The show deals with real-life issues with humour, wisdom and a heart to help and heal people who have gone through challenges in life, as well as helping to restore family values and encourage effective change in communities across the globe for the better.

Part of the change in communities Dilys is involved in is her work with widows. She is the proud founder of the 'Not This Widow Foundation' in Ghana. This foundation helps widows rebuild their lives through financial support and compassion by creating a safe space for them and their children to heal through the grieving process through grief coaching. The foundation helps to facilitate the process by which widows are able to regain their self-confidence and their voice, to empower them to live life on their terms with intention where their voices have been lost through harmful familial, religious, cultural or traditional practices.

Dilys is also the first patron of Fountain of Youth International School in Ghana.

Conscious Dreams
PUBLISHING

Transforming diverse writers
into successful published authors

www.consciousdreamspublishing.com

authors@consciousdreamspublishing.com

Let's connect

www.ingramcontent.com/pod-product-compliance
Lightning Source LLC
Chambersburg PA
CBHW071259110526
44591CB00010B/717